MORE THAN A DOCTOR

More Than a Doctor

THE EXTRAORDINARY LIFE OF
SAMUEL ULYSSES RODGERS

BY ROSALYN RODGERS MOORE

NEW DEGREE PRESS

MORE THAN A DOCTOR
The Extraordinary Life of Samuel Ulysses Rodgers

ISBN   979-8-88504-596-4   *Paperback*
           979-8-88504-942-9   *Kindle Ebook*
           979-8-88504-830-9   *Ebook*

"Everybody thought he was a physician— but really, he was the social change artist who allowed us to make everything a bit fairer."

—JIM NUNNELLY

Table of Contents

Author's Note

I spent much of my time and life in the enjoyment of my father, Samuel U. Rodgers, MD, MPH, a visionary African American doctor of obstetrics and gynecology who transformed health care delivery in Kansas City, Missouri. He achieved endless personal and medical feats throughout his life. His many "first" accomplishments set him apart as he blazed the trail for many others. In 1967, Dr. Rodgers led the planning and administration of the first federally funded community health center in Missouri.

These frequent achievements had almost become the "wallpaper" of my family's life, as the Rodgers family unit achieved multiple "firsts" within various fields of endeavor. They were not without peril during the Jim Crow South era and beyond. However, they found it necessary to make the effort notwithstanding the perils confronting them. Just as no train arrives at the station unmanned, my father did not arrive at his destination alone. His story is told through the lives of his ancestors and shows how ethical leaders are influenced by established family values. My father's ancestor's heroism and achievements provided a foundation for his future successes. He was ultimately described as a man of goodness, mercy, and love. These accomplishments had somehow become our family's "normal," yet they were nothing less than extraordinary given the times during which they happened.

My father had gone places where many would not, demanding that the system do more. "He was a modest but remarkably effective health care reformist," his former administrator summarized. Dr. Sam Rodgers was an innovator, reform-minded physician, trailblazer, risk taker, and barrier breaker.

On the evening of September 15, 2018, I traveled home to participate in the Fiftieth Anniversary Gala Celebration of the Samuel U. Rodgers Health Center (SURHC), a commemorative and fundraising event. It was a celebration like none other for many reasons. The celebration was held in the magnificent Loew's Midland Theatre, an architectural gem constructed in downtown Kansas City in 1927. It was a splendid structure built in the French and Italian Baroque styles, replete with crystal chandeliers and thousands of feet of gold leaf woodwork. The celebration was supported by the who's who of Kansas City commerce, community, health center alumni, administrative and medical staff, friends, and family. It was a bedazzling night with musical entertainment, dinner, and formally attired patrons expressing heartfelt tributes.

Throughout the evening I had several flashbacks of my father's journey. This celebratory venue was a far cry from the beginning days of the health center—then a fledgling dream on untested ground first established in the vacated inner-city projects, characterized by "plywood boarded" windows, bullet-riddled doors, and urine-stained elevator cars. I imagined it was 1968 again and remembered holding my father's hand tightly as we took the elevator up, entering a small odorous concrete block room that served as his temporary office. I had wondered, *Why here?* Had my father responded, I imagine him saying, "Why not here, among the people who need us the most?" Few people knew that his lifetime of dedication stemmed from an impressionable childhood. The son of a small-town doctor, he witnessed firsthand the needs of the poor. Their desperate cries—in the still of the night from his parents' front porch—were never forgotten and were prioritized over fame and fortune.

This brand new, state-of-the-art, federally funded health center was one not experienced in most major cities, much less in the inner city for an indigent population where most dreams die or people just simply stop dreaming. The sleek glass structure was outfitted with the latest medical diagnostic equipment, a clinic organized by specialty, and a staff of compassionate clinicians prepared to treat each patient with respect in their familiar native tongue.

I normally attended these milestone celebrations with my father. That night, he was here only in spirit. Had he lived to experience this night surrounded by the lives he touched, he would have been 101 years old. My sister "Dr. Rita" and I, normally attending proud daughters, were among the keynote speakers. Hundreds gathered to honor his medical accomplishments and most importantly to pay tribute to this man of the times—a good man who led with compassion, integrity, and courage. His personal qualities were drawing cards for many who followed his early vision, and they were not forgotten. Dr. Rodgers tried and true reputation of success inspired many to walk away from their jobs—on a moment's notice—at his mere invitation to commit to a much worthier mission. A mission that would transform attitudes and heal not only bodies, but the soul of a marginalized community.

Life with my father taught me that his success story went well beyond his apparent professional capabilities and accolades. There was more to the story that helped make his dream a reality, that catapulted his mission to the forefront of national public health circles with serendipitous timing. As Rita and I stood off stage—nervously clasping hands prior to our appearance before hundreds—only we knew our father's true essence could not be distilled in minutes. What does it take, first, to make a dream come to life; and how do you keep the vision alive long after the visionary is gone?

Today, people of color and the poor are too often disregarded and considered as less than human or often not seen at all, their contributions to the broader society ignored and their gains destroyed. Their path to achievement actively blocked by barriers of racism or attitudes of indifference.

The representation of African American physicians in health care is one such example.

"The proportion of physicians who are Black in the United States has increased by only 4 percentage points over the past 120 years; and the share of doctors who are Black men remains unchanged since 1940."

"These findings demonstrate how slow progress has been, and how far and fast we have to go if we care about the diversity of the

physician workforce and the health benefits such diversity brings to patients, particularly minority patients."

All people deserve respect based on their sheer humanity and want compassion and opportunity. A vision without total inclusion will languish and become self-serving of the visionary.

Exclusion from social benefits for a targeted group of individuals is a zero-sum game for everyone, as defined by Merriam-Webster dictionary: a fruitless action where "one person or group can win something only by causing another person or group to lose it." (Merriam-Webster Dictionary.)

These extenuating circumstances call on the courage of upcoming generations to raise moral and ethical leaders through positive examples in the days to come.

Numerous news publications extensively chronicled the public life of Dr. Rodgers.

One such editor chose to highlight the importance of - yet difficulty of finding – individuals of exceptionally good character. The inspirational article "Heaven-Sent: Local Heroes Glorify Kansas City" (Ingram's Magazine-December 1996) featured eight Kansas Citians who exhibited this rare quality. In my father's characteristic candor, he was quoted as saying:

"Poor people do not have a chance. If you're not going to help them, then who in the hell is?"

DR. SAMUEL U. RODGERS

Yet few people knew the ultimate measure of this man. As his eldest daughter, I desire to offer a near-complete story derived from long-ago family memories, personal experiences, and multiple interviews of individuals who played a major role in my father's life, success, and development.

Spoiled by my father's commonsense approach to life coupled with good character, I was ill prepared for the lack of such qualities in the leadership I encountered when I entered the workforce. I wondered out loud, "Why are so many crazy people in charge?" "Because people are willing to do whatever it takes to get there and stay there," he resolutely said. His answer would serve me for a lifetime.

This is the story of an unsung hero who dedicated his life to the service of the "least" of these in a forgotten community, without the expectation of accolades or public praise.

It is only through the eyes and memories of many that I can nearly complete this puzzle and share these stories, in hopes of providing readers with the ample courage and a pathway to pursue their own dreams.

Through my sister Rita and my joint recollections as the sole survivors of our immediate family, I write our family story given a front-row seat to these histories. Always curious, my father would expect me to share his truth he lived out daily. We were fortunate to be born into a family of pioneers and life-dedicating servants who became change agents in their communities during pivotal times in this nation for African Americans. Our father, a great and principled man, overcame great adversity and willingly shared his talents to transform a community through compassionate health care delivery. For history's accounting, the benefit of others, and the continued life of his efforts and vision, I must share these stories because they represent the truth as it happened. Let the truth be known, speak for itself, and in so doing, set you free.

The timing of this writing was fortuitous and occasioned by many stops and starts. Too much is at stake to not share the lessons learned, celebrate this victory, and pay it forward for the benefit of the generations to come. As memories fade and the number of original pioneers decrease, the urgency to cultivate their secrets of success increases. SURHC continues to thrive in the role of community and life transformation, with numerous plans still to be realized.

Our lives are inextricably interwoven; we each touch multiple lives. It takes a village, a community of people, and the commitment to principles that form who we become.

Visions are often abandoned due to lack of commitment or courage, or they die along with the visionary. However, based on Dr. Rodgers' lifetime achievements, long-standing progress is only born, carried out, and maintained through courageous and selfless leadership.

This book is for families striving to develop character and instill family values in children through the examples of honesty, integrity, and truth, who wonder if their efforts will make a difference. Childhood is a fertile ground in which seeds of compassion and service can first be planted and take root, sprouting lifetime compass values that filter right from wrong. It is for organizations seeking to establish longevity of purpose and vision.

This book is for medical organizations (medical school deans and students, medical archivists) who believe health care delivery to marginalized communities can and must be improved. It is for government entities (elected officials, city planners, strategists) whose interests are uplifting people and transforming communities.

This book is for the historians who seek community reform blueprints of success.

Lastly, I trust this book will continue to inspire the dream carriers: the dedicated SURHC board members, donors, and staff who keep Dr. Rodgers' vision of compassionate care alive.

As my sister so eloquently stated during her keynote speech, "Dr. Samuel Rodgers' life, unwavering inclusive vision, and work offer hope, a proven roadmap and strategies for health equality—especially needed at a time in history when we are all witnessing the devastating effects of health disparities and the need for a comprehensive public health approach that is available to all people."

"The knowledge of the lived work of this remarkable man continues to provide the impetus for breaking down barriers to health care for the most underserved in our communities, with heart and compassion."

DR. RITA RODGERS STANLEY

For those who seek proof that leadership with integrity based on deep rooted values can leave transformative footprints in the sands of history, this book is for you.

EARLY FAMILY LIFE & EDUCATION (1850–1942)

The Seed

It is only through recent conversations with my second Cousin Horace Jackson Rodgers, now the oldest living patriarch of our family, that many integral parts of the family story have been knitted together. These remembrances were shared at our 2017 family reunion held on Grayhaven Island (Detroit, Michigan) from July 28 to 29. At dusk, on July 29, we lounged on the waterfront patio enjoying each other's company. Our last family reunion was in 1991 in Montgomery, Alabama. We have lost many family members since then. In the quietness of the sunset, we coaxed Cousin Horace to share a few memories as we awaited dinner, and in that split moment I fumbled, then hit "record" on my phone. The listening family members would learn more in this storytelling moment than we had ever known before. Cousin Horace, now ninety-one, remained a treasure trove of detailed family information. I cherished our following phone conversations, deciding to informally document these stories for family eyes only, lest they soon be forgotten.

WETUMPKA, ALABAMA HISTORY

My family's American story began in Wetumpka, Alabama in the 1800s, as far as we can discern. Based on family folklore, Spencer Alexander Rodgers was the first family member born in the United States and the great-grandfather of Samuel U. Rodgers (SUR). He lived, for an unknown period, in an area eventually organized in 1866 and named Wetumpka (Elmore County). Wetumpka, a Muscogee (Creek Native American) phrase *we-wau tum-cau*, meant "rumbling waters" thought to describe the sound of the nearby Coosa River—a river that would loom large in the life of the Rodgers family in the next generation.

This was a land that had experienced campaigns of Native American removal, most notably the 1830 Trail of Tears, and the settlement of Native American land by whites. Over time, forests were replaced with cotton plantations worked by black slaves. 1830 was also a significant milestone for the Rodgers clan, ushering in the birth of its first American son, Spencer. During the Civil War years (1861–1865), Wetumpka experienced the devastation witnessed throughout most of the South but struggled, survived, and eventually grew.

It was into this world that SUR's great-grandfather Spencer Alexander Rodgers and grandfather "Alec" Joseph "AJ" Rodgers were born.

If people can empathize with and inhabit the spirits of others, I believe it was now my family's turn to create and inherit something good out of these ravaged lands. Regardless, it was the land that called my family forth and the land that my family chose to call home. Thinking of my great-grandfather AJ, a scripture arose in my spirit.

Rev. AJ Rodgers Bible

"If you are willing and obedient, you shall eat the good of the land."
ISAIAH 1:19 KJV

THE SEED:

"Spencer Alexander Rodgers, a slave, was SUR's great-grand-father," Cousin Horace recalled. "We come from the Alec J. Rodgers family, all of us."

- Wife: Lucy (1825–unknown), maiden name unknown
- Daughter: Angeline Rodgers (1856–unknown)
- Son: Alexander (Alec) Joseph Rodgers (1858–1919)

Cousin Horace's sole remembrance of our great-great-grand-father, as learned from family, was "Spencer would sit around in the backyard under a tree" in his later years. Census records show that he had a wife "Lucy," although nobody has family memories to share about her life. I imagine my great-great-grandfather now had time to recall all he had suffered, lost, and endured as a slave. The time to suppress or relive memories of the brutality—impossible and painful to do, as he most likely "wore" every insult on his back—and the black skin he could never escape.

Infant slaves—or worse, adult slaves—were separated from their family, never to know each other. The phantom screams of others tortured through rape, beatings, lynchings. The silence of a heart torn apart through daily violation of the human spirit. The smell of blood, sweat, burnt flesh, and the stench of inhumane living conditions. The taste of tears that never stopped flowing. The smell of fear that never went away. The loss of original family birth names and culture, and the frustrating inability to settle the score. It required fortitude to survive. Not much more was known about Spencer. At the end of his life, Spencer lived with his granddaughter, Lucretia Rodgers.

REV. ALEXANDER JOSEPH RODGERS (1858–1919; PLACE OF BIRTH UNKNOWN):

Alec Rodgers, like his father Spencer, was born into slavery. Alec was three years old when the Civil War began and seven years old when slavery and the war ended in 1865. It was in the little city of Wetumpka, framed against the picturesque backdrop of the Appalachian Mountain foothills, that Alec married Amanda Bugg and had four children—two daughters and two sons. It was said that Amanda, originally from Wetumpka, could pass as white, a description used for people racially designated as "mulatto" on the United States census between 1850 and 1930. The term is accordingly defined in the United States as a person who has a white and a black parent.

Alec and Amanda's youngest son, Gordon Rodgers, Sr., would eventually marry Fannie Mamie Lewis, who would become parents to Samuel U. Rodgers.

All four children's educational attainment went well beyond high school. Horace explained, "The entire Rodgers family could read and write, and Alec and his wife, Amanda, corresponded with their four children when they went away to school."

Wife:

- Amanda Bugg (1859–unknown)

Children of Rev. Alexander Joseph Rodgers:

- Lucretia Rodgers (1880–1965), music teacher
- Ulysses Naomi Rodgers (1882–1971), schoolteacher
- Gordon Alexander Rodgers, Sr. (1884–1969), physician, pharmacist, father of Samuel U. Rodgers
- Julian Paris Rodgers, Sr. (1886–1968), attorney, judge

Having learned to read and write was a significant achievement for both the teacher and the student. These actions came with great risk as it was illegal to teach slaves how to read or write; and states passed statutes outlawing these activities. Hearing these stories, I knew my family was courageous and determined to have life in its fullness, preparing for their best futures apart from the risk. This would be just the beginning of my family's association of literacy with liberation and self-esteem. This association would drive migration and moves throughout generations of the Rodgers family. Education was the key to freedom and became a core family value.

"Education was seen by those enslaved as freedom from ignorance and freedom from a menial existence. Seeking literacy was a personal, communal, and political demonstration of resistance to degradation and bondage. Reading the Bible helped the slaves to gain a sense of freedom long before most of them would actually be free of physical chains." (Pg 2. The

History and Heritage of African American Churches—A Way Out of No Way. Author: L. H. Whelchel, Jr.).

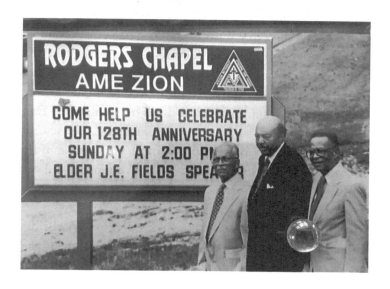

Rodgers Chapel AME Zion, 128th anniversary - Samuel, Horace, Gordon, Jr.

RODGERS CHAPEL AME ZION CHURCH— WETUMPKA, ALABAMA

Cousin Horace continued: "The church was established in 1863, by former slaves with no specific physical meeting place. Alec Rodgers changed his name to Alexander when he became a reverend." Alec, a slave name given at birth, was replaced with Alexander, a Christian name meaning "one who assists men." In 1883, Reverend Alexander J. Rodgers donated the land, and in 1884 the first church structure, Rodgers Chapel AME Zion, was built under his leadership in the center of town. Twenty years later, it was destroyed by a tornado.

In 1886, Wetumpka was struck by two natural disasters: a devastating flood that overran the west bank of Wetumpka and the downtown district, followed by an earthquake that same year. Horace proudly said, "Floods washed out their home and the church, which was moved to higher ground. The church still stands today and has been improved from a church on stilts, so floods won't damage it. The church, rebuilt on stilts to avoid flood damage, is now one of the oldest Christian churches in the city of Wetumpka, still very active in the community."

The Rodgers Chapel was reconstructed at 609 W. Bridge Street, five city blocks west of the "East Bridge Street" that crosses the powerful and beautiful Coosa River.

AJ's pastoral experience in Wetumpka was character building. The strength it took to rebuild after a flood and earthquake had not only transformed AJ's spirit and deepened his faith; his leadership and dedication were noticed by church elders in other places. AJ was asked to pastor a much larger AME church in Montgomery, Alabama. The Rodgers family of six moved to Montgomery, Alabama, seventeen miles away.

OLD SHIP AME ZION CHURCH—MONTGOMERY, ALABAMA
Cousin Horace recalled, "AJ walked every day from Wetumpka to Montgomery." Sometime between 1915 to 1918, AJ Rodgers became a presiding elder of the Old Ship of Zion Church in Montgomery Alabama, the largest AME church

in the United States at the time, apart from the founding church in New York.

October 30, 2021—Atlanta, Georgia: I sat down early Saturday morning to review my documentation of prior phone conversations with Horace. I organized my interview notes into categorized piles, for ease of reference. In the shuffle of papers, a year-old interview comment from Cousin Horace-caught my eye. The note read, "Rodgers Chapel AME Zion (Wetumpka)—Old Church of Zion (Montgomery)...." How had I overlooked a second church in Montgomery? I pulled this Montgomery thread and walked through a door of new understandings. It was the key to the castle in my understanding of my family's early commitment to community activism. The Montgomery church history was there for the asking, documented on multiple historical websites. My anticipation grew at fever pitch with every found article.

Finally, my heart skipped a beat when I spotted the name "AJ Rodgers" listed among thirty-three African American pastors beginning in 1862 through today. I cupped my hands over my mouth and just rested in breathless disbelief, with tear-filled eyes. This was my first documented evidence—apart from verbal family histories—that AJ was there in a big way. He was present in a place that actively had influenced so many lives, as his descendants would come to do as well. This discovery made me want to know more.

DR. A. J. RODGERS
Presiding Elder, A. M. E. Zion Church
1918

AJ Rodgers Presiding Elder, AME Zion Church, 1918

I learned that Old Zion was listed by the Birmingham Civil Rights Institute as among the twenty places that changed the world, along with twenty-five other Alabama Civil Rights sites known to be at the epicenter of the African American Civil Rights Movement. According to the Net Ministries Old Ship A.M.E. Zion Church history accounts, the church was "rolled on logs to its present location on Holcomb Street near Mildred Street" in 1852 and named Old Ship Zion Church, a gift from white parishioners. Today, it is described as "a monument to the courageous, devoted souls of the past and a source of inspiration and constant challenge to the noblest in religion and culture."

On March 3, 1976, Old Zion was placed on the Alabama Register of Landmarks and Heritage and the National Register of Historic Places on January 24, 1991. It felt as if my head and heart were simultaneously swelling with knowledge and gratitude as I learned the history of Old Zion.

What I would learn would place me one step closer to understanding the DNA of my family that drew them toward societal issues, igniting their courageous and faithful steps into the unknown to improve the conditions of the invisible with a faith that would wear a boldness amid fears of retaliation, loss of reputation, income, or life. I accepted a long time ago that so much of life—and now this memoir journey—would be revealed by chance, serendipity, and God's timing. This was the root of our family's DNA. This was the "why" that became the motivation of generational accomplishments to come. No family member can separate or disassociate themselves from this truth any more than one can separate the glow from the moon. This acknowledgment drew me even closer.

Built in 1918, the online photograph of Old Zion's interior was impressive. I wondered, in the moment, if my great-grandfather AJ Rodgers had experienced this sanctuary. I wanted to believe that he had. After additional research, I learned he had become the presiding elder in 1919.

I committed to be there physically inside this sanctuary one day soon. Even through just this photograph, I felt the power and grace that had been ordained for many in this space. I imagined the reverberating oratory that filled the air, giving daily sustenance to people whose lives were diminished every day through no fault of their own. I was already there in spirit, wanting to know and feel that inspirational vibe that protected our great-grandfather—that force that gave him enough life to fulfill his part of the relay race to ultimately pass that baton of courage and purpose with such force that it would sustain and propel his descendants for generations to come. Though physically separated from this inspirational place, I felt the soulful embrace of a make-believe choir and congregation as verses from "Go Down Moses" played in my head.

Go down, Moses, way down in Egypt land
Tell old Pharaoh to let my people go

So, Moses went to Egypt land
Let my people go
He made old Pharaoh understand
Let my people go

On Saturday, November 27, 2021, I traveled to Montgomery, Alabama for a funeral and decided afterwards to visit the "Old Zion" church. I stood outside the historic edifice imagining all the life-changing miracles that must have occurred within these walls.

National Register of Historic Places

2021 Visit to Old Zion

AJ Rodgers became a Reverend of the Methodist denomination that freed slaves through community activism, valued women's leadership; and became the church known for "speaking truth to power." He was committed to the greater good of the community while building and modeling the moral core of his family by instilling values in his children through his lived example. He was a freedom fighter and a family man. I believe he knew there could be no progress made in human affairs without first having the "right heart" to pursue and influence these issues. His faith was in the power of love for all, regardless of race or gender.

I believe this activist background that required truth telling, integrity, courage, bravery, and the concern for the betterment of others became the springboard that would launch future generations of the Rodgers family.

I contend the problems that plague this nation today—having existed since its founding—is the rott of the human heart and the selfish ego of power that has grown undeterred in its place. It takes humility then certainty to change a course of action midstream. This moral compass was the embryonic seed fertilized and watered by challenges, steadfast prayer, and fortitude that would protect and open unexpected doors during the most impossible of times for the future generations of the Rodgers clan but only for those courageous enough to test the times.

Family stories record that Reverend AJ Rodgers fell from a ladder doing roof repairs of the "Old Zion" church at age sixty-one. He died in 1919, two years after the birth of his grandson, Sam Rodgers, having lived in committed service to his family, church, and community.

AJ Rodgers had chosen to be in the forefront, an outspoken proponent of civil rights and the major societal issues of the day in his community. AJ had achieved the impossible in those times by overcoming the adversity placed in his path. What would the Rodgers family risk for the promise of the potential fulfillment of their dreams and hopes?

The Harvest

SUR'S BIRTH FAMILY

Growing up in the South in the 1900s was different for different people. My father, Samuel Ulysses Rodgers, was named at birth on August 10, 1917, in his parents' home on 1618 Cooper Avenue, Anniston, Alabama. He was born into an educated, entrepreneurial, enterprising, and trailblazing family. These accomplishments, rare at any time in the lives of African Americans, were certainly unfathomable in the times they occurred. It is the "puzzling duality" of this "seeming impossibility" that render my father and his family's life stories as nothing short of amazing.

The heart and nature of the Rodgers clan were of strength, compassion, and integrity. A quiet determination and a reserved personality prevailed. A veiled strength, an unspoken oath to accomplish what needed to be done regardless of self-sacrifice. There was no unproductive household drama to distract from one's goal—only a clear expectation that you would do your best, not solely for you but also for the benefit of others. Education was the law of the land. "I knew that I would go to college; it was just a matter of when and where," my father would often say with a chuckle. Disrespect for anyone was a cardinal sin. This family gained advantageous opportunity as they actively chose to open doors previously shut or gratefully walked through doors already opened because they believed they could. They listened, were led, and proceeded on faith and through grace, preparedness, and serendipity, made history. My father's life could not have been without the family gifts of character modeled for him.

1919 Rodgers siblings and mother at park

Rodger's siblings and Mother at Home

Preceded in life by his sister, Frances Elouise, and brother, Gordon Alexander, he was positioned by birth order to receive extra attention as the baby of the family. Both parents were business owners and community servants. His father, Gordon Alexander Rodgers, Sr., was a physician, and his mother, Fannie Mamie Lewis-Rodgers, a home maker. The roots of the Rodgers family began in small town Alabama (Wetumpka, Montgomery, Anniston) as far as can be traced. The journey from the African continent is unknown.

If families possess common character traits, the Rodgers could be described as peaceful, steady, caring people of integrity. The family disposition and temperament were one of calm deliberation. We courageously approached many moments of historic urgency throughout our lives. Never once did we hear our father raise his voice. He reserved that level of ire for institutional failures in systems that didn't protect and care for people.

Rev. AJ Rodgers

Samuel found many examples in his family. The seed of our family was Samuel's grandfather, Reverend Alexander Joseph Rodgers. Throughout the family lineage, there are what I have observed and deemed "the spirited pair" personality combination. This calm, unflappable, still-waters-run-deep personality paired with the excitable, push-the-envelope characteristic made for an effective combination. Often these distinctly different traits would morph from one person to another. Regardless of one's natural bent, the spirited pair duality shared common traits and pivoted on each other's strengths. The common thread was a heart for people, guided by integrity with developed good character—all contributed by each generation. Family sightings of the spirited pair include:

MEMORABLE SIBLING DUOS

Dr. Gordon Alexander Rodgers, Sr. / Julian Paris Rodgers, Esquire

Dr. Samuel Ulysses Rodgers / Dr. Gordon Alexander Rodgers, Jr.

Rosalyn Rodgers Moore / Dr. Rita Rodgers Stanley

Dr. and Mrs. Gordon A. Rodgers, Sr. created an exemplary life for their children and contributed to their community, all while thriving in the pressure-cooking stew of the Jim Crow South.

Dr. Gordon Alexander Rodgers, Sr.

CAUTIOUS BUT UNDETERRED

Our family traveled every summer from Kansas City, Missouri, to Anniston, Alabama. We traveled by train in the 1950s, by station wagon in the '60s, and finally in a thirty-five-foot motor home in the late '70s and early '80s. My father would drive roughly 800 miles one way nonstop, the result of Jim Crow laws that did not allow African Americans to stay in hotels or to use "whites-only" facilities. We somehow found non-hostile gas stations along the way that would allow us to buy gas and use the toilet facilities.

Prior to the passage of the 1964 Civil Rights Act, travel could be difficult and dangerous. In 1936, "The Negro Motorist Green Book" was created by Victor Green, a Black postal worker who lived in Harlem, New York City. The Green Book became the travel guide of the '40s, '50s, and '60s, providing a listing of safe havens (hotels, gas stations, drug stores, restaurants etc.) for African Americans. Washington, DC, had more listings than any other city. My father had a personal network of friends spanning the country who provided safe havens and so much more. This network began early in his student years at Talladega, Alabama, carrying through his medical school years at Howard University. We stayed at the homes of his personal friends when traveling anywhere but to Anniston, all outstanding individuals both professionally and personally. They were fascinating and shared their life journeys. I wanted to be in their presence, in the midst of a generation that had overcome much.

It was a twelve-hour journey with three young children and no air conditioning, which was commonplace in those days. There were no computer games or GPS systems. My mother prepared fried chicken, deviled eggs, fruit, and miscellaneous snacks. My siblings and I thought it was the best adventure. We didn't have to sit up straight at the dinner table fully dressed. Instead, we removed our white polished Keds tennis shoes, ate, and played games, all while sitting cross-legged in the bucket seat that faced backward. We sang, read, napped, and counted horses, pigs, and cows along the highway.

My father, armed with several AAA maps and the courage and stamina to drive through the 1960s South, had a much greater purpose in mind. He was cautious but undeterred by what we might encounter, as we traveled mostly highway, with a few small-town detours. He wanted us to experience his birth home of Anniston and the special people and environment that shaped him. He wanted us to know "our people." He was a purposeful and strategic man always, and this was no exception. My father's purpose was fulfilled as those family bonds he hoped for are as strong as ever today. We consider our first cousins as brothers and sisters. We remain loyal and supportive of each other still, and the years gone by have only strengthened the bonds. We are grateful for the foundation laid over sixty years ago—now forever unbreakable. My generation is now "on call" to "pay forward" all that our ancestors continue to be to us.

We spent a month of our summer vacation in Anniston, surrounded by first cousins, aunts, uncles, and doting grandparents. We loved Anniston; it was a small town you could get your arms around as a kid. Our daily schedule was comprised of multiple trips between my uncle Gordon's home on Claxton Street and my grandparents' home on Cooper Avenue, with visits to Miss Pete's Variety Store for rounds of syrup-flavored snow cones. We ate at both ends of our trek, and greeted everyone along the way, southern style; respectfully speaking to everyone—whether we knew them or not. We splashed around almost daily at the segregated swimming pool. Often our carefree lives were permeated with parental requirements to participate in mass meetings and civil rights marches, common in this deep South city. Though childishly disappointed about our missed swims, I am beyond grateful for the parental insistence to participate in a much bigger movement. The adults exposed yet protected us from the festering racial issues of the day. There was no sugar coating of the realities of black life in this country. We were expected to participate.

In downtown Anniston, Noble Street ran through the main shopping area of Anniston and the tree-lined residential boulevards. Quintard Boulevard became my emotional gateway to the experiences that would lie ahead—our cue to sit up, smooth our hair, brush away crumbs, and straighten our clothing. Once my father made that slow and careful left turn onto 15th Street, we had truly crossed over to the proverbial other side of the track—the gateway to the black community. 15th Street was lined with African American barber shops, laundromats, beauty parlors, and bicycle shops. Within minutes we would pass my grandparents' church (First Congregational) that sat up on the hill. My heart raced with excitement as I knew the next memorized turn would be a right onto Cooper Avenue. We eased slowly uphill toward 1618 located mid-way up the block. At the top of the hill stood the 17th Street Baptist Church at 801 West 17th Street. Our sky blue, bug-covered station wagon eased into the narrow driveway that separated my grandparents' house (1618

Cooper Avenue) from my Uncle Gordon's dental practice, established in the house next door at 1616 Cooper Avenue.

1618 COOPER AVENUE

My grandparents built a house next door to their primary residence where their son (Gordon A. Rodgers, Jr.) would practice dentistry for over forty years, and now their granddaughter (Dr. Beverly C. Rodgers) who practices there twice a week. I understood instantly having spent time in my grandparents' home that my father had not coincidentally "happened upon" this bent to be purposeful and strategic; it was learned.

Now in the common driveway nestled between the Rodgers enclave of houses—car doors flung open—the 1618 Cooper residents (cousins, Aunt Elouise, and grandparents) instantly appeared on the front porch, descended the steps traversing the small front lawn, pouring into the driveway in seconds. It was this bee swarm-like blanket of love that would begin and end every Anniston visit. Consequently, the reverse was also unavoidable; as our summer visits inevitably came to an end, our departures and goodbyes were slow and prolonged, filled with tears, laughter, and hugs.

BBQS, BIRTHDAY PARTIES, AND MORE

My sister Rita, born August 5, celebrated every birthday until her eighteenth in my grandparents' backyard in Anniston. My father, born August 10, was more than happy to fade into the background of this August festivity. My sister's birthday party was the fête of the summer season for six-year-olds, almost bigger than the Fourth of July. My grandmother knew everyone in town. Every child close to my sister's age from church and the neighborhood was invited. She happily planned and organized every detail of the party. There was no such thing as pants-wearing for special occasions such as these. All the little girls arrived in dresses to run through the backyard, awaiting their turn on the sliding board or in other games. Overcome by the heat and the excitement of the day, the belle of the birthday ball was summoned indoors, with flushed cheeks, to rest and hydrate on the chaise lounge. She had the immediate attention of three doctors—Doctors Gordon Sr., Gordon Jr., and Samuel Rodgers—indoors enjoying the BBQ, homemade cake, and ice cream. All ended well, and the partygoers looked forward to Rita's return visit every summer.

We relished our summer visits. On the return leg of the trip back to Kansas City, our cooler was packed with Aunt Weese's (Elouise) homemade pimento cheese, ham salad, and fig jam. As my father reversed the blue station wagon slowly out of the driveway, my Anniston family drew near. As the car went into drive, my Anniston family ran out into the middle of the street, walking then running while waving until the blue station wagon was out of sight. Today, we laugh about our trademark goodbyes; some things never change.

Every year our entire family took what we called the "step picture." Summer after summer- we lined up from the bottom step to the top. The first row was reserved for Grandmommy; always cradling the newest addition. Being surrounded by her eleven grandchildren was her heaven on earth. The sizable collection of "step photos" chronicles the growth of our family. We were blanketed and protected by this love from the beginning to the end of our Anniston visits; more importantly it continues to guide the Rodgers clan wherever we go.

Before my brother and sister and I went away to college, our family had traveled to every state in the union with exception of Rhode Island and Hawaii; driving all the way. We traveled to San Francisco, the Grand Canyon, the White House, and the Statue of Liberty in New York City. I don't know if my father utilized the Green Book, as he could rely on enjoyed friendships from the east to the west coasts.

LAKE GATHERINGS

In the 1960s, the Rodgers clan gatherings occurred mostly in Anniston, with short day trips taken to Montgomery, Alabama, to visit Aunts Ulysses and Lucretia or picnicking at Guntersville Dam, Guntersville, Alabama; a highlight for the many family fishermen and women. In the summer of 1963, our grandparents hosted the Rodgers clan at Kentucky Lake. My grandparents rented cottages for each family unit, all expenses paid. I remember all eleven first cousins gathered there, with their respective families. We were "stair step" first cousins beginning with the birth of Frances Elaine in 1942 through the birth of Michelle Elizabeth in 1963. In beautiful Kentucky Lake, my father patiently taught me and Rita how to swim on our backs. That summer we gained instant credibility from our older brother, Rickey, already an avid and proficient swimmer. It was worth the few gulps of the lake.

Regardless of educational achievements and societal contributions, life remained segregated in the Jim Crow South. In

Anniston, sixteen movie theaters established between 1883 and 1983 for white patrons all located on Noble Street. Three colored theaters were established between 1917 and 1945, all located on West 15th Street, the business heart of the African American community. There were white and black baseball teams, schools, businesses, pools, churches, and health care. This was the community into which my father was born. A cross section of hard-working people from laborers to professionals, a village with the purpose of raising and nurturing the African American children of the community. Encouraging them to dream to be all they could be and protecting them to the extent possible against the harsher realities of life in this country. Regardless of outside and repressive forces, this African American community rose to the occasion.

In 1968, during a summer visit to Anniston, I had a movie-going experience like never before. As we arrived at the downtown movie theater, my Anniston cousins instructed me to follow them as they climbed the exterior fire escape ladder. I hesitantly followed regarding it as a prank. I learned as we entered the second level of the theater that this was the route to the "colored only" section of the theater, the only place we were allowed to sit.

I realized this world saw me differently than I saw myself. I understood clearly that this other world played by different rules, established for different colored bodies.

The Rodgers Enclave

"It is the family that gives us a deep private sense of belonging. Here we first begin to have our self—defined for us."

—HOWARD THURMAN

This same north star of our male ancestors, Spencer and Alexander Rodgers, influenced, formed, guided, and blessed the next generation, even when they were least aware.

In the confines of my grandparents' home at 1618 Cooper (a full house of five adults and seven children during summer visits) you could learn, hear, and see a lot, in a civically minded family. The number of family members could easily swell to eighteen when the other Rodgers within walking distance would drop by throughout the day. My uncle Dr. Gordon A. Rodgers, Jr. had a dental practice next door and would bounce between the houses for lunch or whenever a break was in order. The occasional patient would show up on the front porch unanticipated "looking for Doc Rodgers," they'd say, as pain selected its own moments. It would take a few seconds of triage to figure out which "Doc" was needed, as three "Dr. Rodgers" were available at once.

Family step picture, Anniston, Alabama

This house was a happy and a "happening place," but if boredom ever visited, you had only to plop down in the chair at the picture window, look across the drive and into the dental chair next door to gain a full view of the patient reclined under the blinding overhead spotlight. I learned compassion in those moments, selfishly glad it wasn't my turn in the chair. If your boredom was prolonged and time allowed, you could mosey across the driveway to the dental office. On a slow day, you might charm Dr. Gordon into squirting a pellet of mercury into your palm, where it would roll around as you giggled until it dropped.

Unlike the more serious other two docs, Uncle Gordon could operate in the childlike world of fun, fantasy, and curiosity as if he'd never left. Through his example, Uncle Gordon taught me you could save the world with a cheerful heart, coupled with a lot of courage and determination.

Uncle Gordon and my father were the second-generation example of the "memorable sibling duo," exhibiting these characteristic personality traits and roles throughout their lives. Gordon was the playful sibling, fun-loving and full of surprises, while Samuel was an introspective observer of human nature and behavior and a strategic thinker. A statement written later in a family obituary described Uncle Gordon as "a man of boundless energy, a big heart, indomitable spirit, and intriguing mind."

The brothers shared similar attributes (i.e., courageous and determined community servants) but dissimilar approaches. Gordon would react at once—heart drawn—to an issue with a damn-the-torpedoes, full-steam-ahead approach, and Samuel would quietly and methodically assess the impending challenge, then strategically plan the next steps. Neither brother ever avoided a challenge; instead, they became involved when it was the right thing to do. Gordon was effervescent in expression, Samuel quietly observant. Both were dedicated humanitarian and civil rights soldiers who would alter the trajectory of history in their communities.

In my grandmother's kitchen I would learn humility and that regardless of status, there are rare moments when you should never say no. "No, I don't like this vegetable" or "No, I'd rather not eat that"—not in Fanny Mamie's kitchen. Everyone ate whatever delicacy she dished up, including my dad, the famous doctor from Kansas City who disrupted the status quo of medical politics in health care.

In my grandmother's kitchen I would also learn there are times you remain open in consideration of other options. Here I would learn to love homegrown tomatoes and squash, previously shunned, and say yes. I would practice the art of negotiation and learn that food was also medicine—a way to soothe and heal a broken heart. I would trade collard greens—considered bitter and detestable—for homegrown tomatoes, my reasonable swap and counteroffer. Most importantly, I would witness the strength and beauty of women in the family and community.

I learned that most men were not half as decent as my grandfather. Children easily gravitated toward him, sensing his ease with patients and people after over fifty years of practicing medicine. He called me "Sugar Pie Peaches" and another cousin "Pumpkin." Neither of us will ever know the derivation of those names; it simply made us feel loved and special.

This was the family life we could control. There was another whole life we could not, one that Black people lived in. A challenging and dangerous world not of their making, and the people who made this history knew the least about it—or at least pretended so.

BROTHERS GORDON, SR. AND JULIAN RODGERS

Dr. Gordon Alexander Rodgers, Sr. (1884–1969), and Julian Paris Rodgers (1886–1968), Esq., the sons of Rev. Alexander Rodgers—preacher's kids (PKs)—were the first generation of the Rodgers family born out of slavery, as free people in Wetumpka, Alabama. My grandfather Gordon Sr. would become the first physician in the Rodgers family, beginning the medical branch of the Rodgers family in the South. He was followed by four generations of doctors and dentists that continue today. His brother Julian would begin the legal branch of our family in the Midwest.

Brothers Gordon A. Rodgers, Sr. and Julian P. Rodgers

As described in the book, *Annie's Town Revisited - A Picture History of Anniston, Alabama*, "Dr. Gordon Alexander Rodgers, Sr., a graduate of Meharry Medical College in Nashville, Tennessee, came to Anniston, Alabama in stages. After completing his sophomore year at Meharry and passing the Pharmacology Board Examination, he came to Anniston, where he worked in Dr. Charles Thomas's drug store during the summer." He returned to Anniston at the end of his junior year to the same employment, and upon graduating from Meharry in 1908 at age twenty-four, he made Anniston his permanent home. "In 1910—at the age of twenty-six—he would marry the former Fannie Mamie Lewis, later becoming the parents to Frances Elouise Rodgers (Ransom), Gordon Alexander Rodgers, Jr., and Samuel Ulysses Rodgers." (Annie's Town Revisited, pg. 316)

Gordon A. Rodgers, Sr., Meharry Medical College graduate

My most vivid memory of Julian was in a sepia-colored class photo, Julian was one of two African American children in the photo, surrounded by other young white boys in matching school uniforms. At the bottom of the photograph appeared the name of the boarding school and the year 1908. I held onto that memory for years, not recalling where I had first seen this photograph, and most puzzling of all, never knowing the back story. The circumstance seemed both incredulous and impossible in 1908. Periodically, I would question various cousins, but no one had ever seen this photograph. In 2017, Julian's granddaughter Pamela Rodgers visited Atlanta and became the key to this unsolved mystery. Not only had my Detroit cousin seen the photograph, but she was also remarkably familiar with the photo and history and began to gladly share her grandfather's story. I rushed to hit record on my phone.

Her grandfather was whisked away to Hampton, Virginia in a lifesaving effort to escape threatening circumstances in the Jim Crow South. This newly disclosed leg of the journey was my link to the boarding school photograph. Cousin Horace would later provide more surrounding details than imaginable.

RELIGION AND SPIRITUALITY:
DR. GORDON A. RODGERS, SR. (1884 - 1969)

My grandfather was a quiet, strong, and thoughtful man just like his son, my father. He was an oasis of peace, while enjoying the swirl of family motion around him. He was a gentle giant, remembered by a first cousin Janet Ransom who was raised under his roof as "a man of few words...who said what he meant...and meant what he said." Years later when 1618 Cooper was being cleaned out, Janet discovered a book entitled *As a Man Thinketh*. This self-help classic written by James Allen in 1902 simply concludes, "You are what you think." "The book explores how your thoughts create your circumstances, why having a purpose in life is essential, and how to take control of your mind and your life." (Short Form Book Summary of "As A Man Thinketh" by James Allen")

Gordon, Sr. grew up with the moniker preacher's kid. Years later, the Anniston grandchildren described him as a "spiritual man," who became somewhat disenchanted with and lost patience for organized religion. Janet said, "After he died, I was asked by an inquisitive Annistonian, 'Was he an atheist?' I quickly responded, "No he was spiritual…and he woke up every day of his life and went to church—metaphorically speaking—to improve the lives of others. He was a community servant, who saw many unfulfilled health care needs and committed his life to addressing them."

JULIAN PARIS RODGERS (1886–1968)

Growing up, Gordon, Sr. was clearly the quieter of the two brothers. Julian, the baby of the family—just like his nephew Samuel—had the effervescent playfulness of Samuel's brother Gordon, Jr. Julian and Gordon, Sr. were opposites in demeanor but shared a determination and drive to prosper.

We visited Uncle Julian on rare occasions when we traveled to Detroit, Michigan, during my childhood years. He was kind and funny. I have no recollection of his presence in the old familiar Rodgers clan gathering places (i.e., Wetumpka, Montgomery, Anniston, or Talladega, Alabama). Julian remained absent from our family visits to the South.

At the Rodgers family reunion in Grayhaven Island (Detroit, Michigan; July 28–29, 2017), Cousin Horace proudly shared the story of his father, Julian Paris Rodgers.

It was an honor when Rev. A.J. Rodgers was asked to pastor a larger AME Church in Montgomery, however creating an unexpected family peril. Young Julian, "the rambunctious one," unknowingly defied the laws of the Jim Crow South, by playfully drinking out of the "whites only" fountain. Julian's childish behavior could cost him his life. No exceptions were made for penalties paid by African Americans, whether child or adult.

Later in life, Uncle Julian's ebullient personality and *joie de vivre* carried him to greater heights. However, now was not the time. His parents, unable to break him of this prankish behavior, made a difficult but life preserving decision. Julian was sent away to Hampton Institute in Hampton, Virginia, to continue his elementary school education.

Julian, separated from immediate family, completed both elementary and junior high school at Hampton Institute in 1904, seemingly alone. Fortunately, Julian met classmate Stephen Sparks while at Hampton, beginning a lifelong friendship. Julian excelled at Hampton and received a Hampton administrator's recommendation to attend the prestigious Phillips Exeter Academy (PEA) High School with Exeter's financial support. In Exeter, New Hampshire, Julian and Stephen became two of the first African Americans to attend PEA. Stephen completed his education at Phillips Exeter in 1907, and Julian in 1908. Julian and Stephen became the best of friends, forever, and self-adopted brothers.

"Julian, extremely outgoing, made many more friends at PEA, Henry Morgenthau among them who later became the United States treasurer during the Roosevelt era," Horace explained.

Grace continued to pave Julian's path. Upon completing Exeter, Julian received offers from several East Coast Ivy League schools, including Brown University. Stephen Sparks, then attending the University of Michigan, invited Julian to join him, so that "they might again be the buddies they were at Exeter."

Inseparable friends, Julian completed his undergraduate work at the University of Michigan between 1908 and 1912 and entered the University of Michigan's law school in 1912, finishing in 1915.

In 1915, Julian would meet his bride from Lansing, Michigan, and marry. Julian had survived and thrived, strengthened by his parents' heart-wrenching decision and prayers. Along with his brother, this memorable sibling duo were poised to conquer the world. Julian rejoined his birth family in Montgomery, Alabama, after departing over a decade ago. It was now time to pass the Alabama bar.

THE MICHIGAN AND ALABAMA BAR

Graduation from a Michigan law school automatically admitted one to the Michigan bar. Julian's ultimate plan was always to return home to Alabama—just as my father would plan decades later. The best made plans often go awry.

Julian, informed by a courthouse clerk that he could not get a bar application, sought the advice of a powerful man, his father. Rev. AJ Rodgers was now the presiding elder of Old Ship Zion AME Church, then the largest AME church in the US. Julian was advised to "go back to the same clerk." Upon Julian's return the same clerk reached under the counter, angrily throwing the paperwork at him and dismissively saying, "Give me ten dollars. It's JUST MORE money...more money for the state of Alabama." Undeterred, Julian completed the application and sat for the Alabama bar, becoming one of the first African American attorneys to take—and pass—the written exam in the state of Alabama.

LAW AND DISORDER

In 1915, Julian volunteered for World War I service and in 1916 joined the army to attend officer candidate school (OCS). Julian was sent to Fort De Moines, promoted from First to Second Lieutenant, and served as an officer in France and Germany. "My parents decided that when my dad returned home from the service, they were moving back to Michigan," Horace said. The young couple had never suffered such indignities as they experienced in the South—unable to try on hats or shoes in the store and so much more. His wife, unwilling to endure the racial hardships of the South, welcomed the return to Detroit.

Julian Paris Rodgers migrated North, once again, and established a private law practice. In 1925, he became the first known African American attorney in the country to become a city attorney. He served as assistant corporate counsel from 1925 to 1951. Horace said, "My father was the first African American to have an office in City Hall, and the second to be employed at City Hall." After an illustrious career, Julian retired from the Assistant Corporation Counsel's Office for the City of Detroit, where he won the largest monetary settlement for a Highland Park water usage case. Sons Julian Paris Rodgers, Jr. and Horace Jackson Rodgers would become attorneys. Generations later, four more members of the Rodgers clan would graduate from the University of Michigan, including Julian's nephew Dr. Samuel U. Rodgers.

Julian's childhood migration from Alabama to Virginia would be the first known example of family separation in the Rodgers clan, to afford their children a most essential commodity: education, as well as a chance to stay alive, in Julian's case. This family's life was disrupted and entangled in the pervasiveness of Jim Crow laws and the vileness of hate. I reflect on the human potential that may have been lost had young Julian not escaped the South. It would not be the Rodgers family's last experience with family separation. When one door closed, they looked for another to open.

Baby Ulysses

Baby Elouise

YOUNG SAMUEL ULYSSES RODGERS (1917–1999)

Young Samuel's mother called him by his middle name "Ulysses" from early on. She pronounced it in a long and drawn-out Southern way: "yoo-luh-seez." In a baby book found among family keepsakes, his mother noted in cursive handwriting the home birth details of the three Rodgers siblings.

- Frances Elouise Rodgers born Saturday, 4:20 p.m., July 5, 1913
- Gordon Alexander Joseph Rodgers, Jr. born Thursday, 2:40 a.m., October 28, 1915
- Samuel Ulysses Rodgers born Friday, 7:30 p.m., August 10, 1917

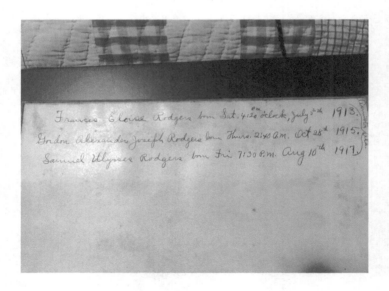

Baby book birthdates

In several studio photographs of the children, Ulysses, the youngest, wore braids up until the age of three or so. It was a common practice at the time to delay cutting a boy's hair. He was a curious child interested in learning about things outside of his parents' home. As a young boy he was known to wander away from the Rodgers home to surrounding neighborhoods. He was already curious about other people, where and how they lived. Occasionally he returned home after these wanderings with a few scrapes and minimal roughing up. I wondered if these scuffles resulted from self-defense, or my father's guardian protection of someone else being bullied.

Rodgers siblings, Russel Studios

Ulysses was left-handed (a southpaw) and had a slight stutter that he eventually outgrew. He was encouraged by parents and teachers to switch dominant hands out of a genuine desire to make a southpaw's life easier in a right-handed world.

All three Rodgers siblings attended elementary school in Anniston, Alabama, for as long as the available education institutions allowed. After the age of twelve, African Americans were without many secondary educational options to further their education locally. The few options included only training schools that would prepare a student for a trade. Dr. and Mrs. Rodgers, progressive in every way, had already planned around this discriminatory practice for their children. It would involve the temporary separation of the five-member family and relocation to Talladega, Alabama. The plan proved faultless, and all three Rodgers siblings completed their secondary education and received college degrees on time.

First Family

INTERVIEW WITH DR. SAMUEL U. RODGERS AND DR. GORDON A. RODGERS, JR.

In the fall of 1998, a small group of family members gathered in the library of the building I still call home, a high-rise condominium in Midtown Atlanta, Georgia. The setting for the interview was the library, a traditionally appointed dark wood-paneled room with wall-to-wall bookshelves and a variety of lounge seating groupings. The recorded interview was the novel idea of a first cousin, who scheduled an interviewer to pose the questions we most wanted to know about the lives of these brothers: Gordon now eighty-three years of age and Samuel eighty-one. Their sister Elouise had passed away in 1994.

They sat side by side in two easy chairs outfitted with ottomans and spoke candidly about their lives. The interviewer asked a variety of questions that included their Anniston childhoods, education, parents, student life, professional careers, military, the Kansas City migration, and their immediate families. The library was cozy quiet as the children of both brothers sat on the edge of their seats in anticipation of what was to come.

Mayfair Library

The brothers' thoughtful responses were occasionally punctuated with the predictable ribbing, irritable impatience, and sibling annoyance that had been hallmarks of this memorable sibling duo throughout their lives. I remain forever thankful for this memorable day that chronicled their lives, in their own words. I wondered, "Why hadn't we taken the time to do this years ago?" Within the next couple years, my brother and father would pass away on the same date, exactly one year apart.

1618 COOPER AVENUE, CHILDHOOD HOME

In 1920, the Rodgers family lived in Anniston, in a section of town without sewer or plumbing on the west side of the railroad tracks. "We at least had a water line, and mother would go out and get water to cook with," Gordon, Jr. proudly said. Some neighbors retrieved water from a well. Every room in the house had a receptacle (a slop jar, two-gallon bucket) for using the bathroom. "I was the slop jar emptier. A bathroom was unheard of on Cooper Avenue in 1920." As eighty-three-year-old Gordon relived this story, he wept like the five-year-old "slop jar emptier" again. This childhood experience was evidently more impactful than any of us had previously known. Surprised, we wondered if he had been mocked by neighboring children.

Rodgers siblings on trikes

In the early 1900s, my father's mother, Fannie Mamie, attended Talladega College under extraordinary circumstances. Josephine Lawler was the woman who raised Fannie Mamie, along with three biological sons Bud, "D," and Sam. These brothers sent their sister to college, as laborers at the Foundry. Fair-skinned Fannie Mamie stood out among these three dark-skinned brothers, raising much speculation—then and now. One brother, a union member who worked in the coal mine, had his house dynamited. He managed to save his piano, unscratched, which now sits in my grandparents' living room at 1618 Cooper.

It was unusual for a black man to become a union member, as Southern whites believed unions promoted integration. What white person would want to help a black person attain better pay?

In 1930, no more than fifty thousand out of 1,500,000 (3.33 percent) black workers were members of any trade union. In 1935, the Congress of Industrial Organizations (CIO) sought to organize industrial workers regardless of race or ethnic background, which helped to alleviate the historic conflict between African Americans and labor unions. (National Archives: African Americans and the American Labor Movement. Federal Records and African American History Summer 1997, Vol. 29, No. 2)

Today there remain questions about the identity of Fannie's father. My father explained that his mother had educational opportunities different from most women in those days and was viewed as a special kid in South Anniston. "She was a child of an interracial relationship and undoubtedly had special privileges and advantages that others didn't have." Fannie received a junior college degree that certified her as a teacher, taught school in Anniston for about a year, and married. It was against the law for black women to acquire a bachelor's degree.

Their mother's unknown life circumstance was an enigma to the brothers. Fannie's children remained amazed that never once during their childhood in the small town of Anniston was the truth of her parentage ever whispered. It was this haunting presence of his mother's parental uncertainty that my father could never forget.

Today I hold in my hand my grandmother's locket, a great discovery found as we packed her house. The round gold locket with diagonal crisscross scoring on the back was dotted at every intersected line with small blue zircon birthstones, totaling sixteen. The front was engraved with her scripted initials, FML. I gasped when I forced the locket open, revealing a foggy black-and-white photo of a man. I know no more than my father did, but I have a piece of her in my heart that adorns my neck. Decades later, on occasion, the latest rumor surfaces. I believe this was her father, her birthstone, and her sweet sixteen birthday gift. A classic black-and-white photo of my grandmother hangs in the foyer of my home. She is photographed standing proudly with the locket resting on her breast. I wondered if she knew of her biological father all the while.

Young Fannie Mamie, FML locket

PROFESSIONAL LIFE OF FANNIE MAMIE LEWIS RODGERS

Grandmother Fannie Mamie had a sense for business. She was considered and respected by the men in her house and by the community as an entrepreneurial spirit. She was directive-driven and always had a plan for herself and everyone else in case they didn't. I believe she thought idle hands were an opportunity waiting to be filled, and there were so many useful things to be done. She was "constant motion" in her aproned house dress, sweeping both back and front porches, hanging wet clothes on the line, or making desserts daily. These activities were wedged between her civic and community activities where she clearly dressed to be taken seriously.

Mrs. Fannie Mamie Lewis Rodgers, dressed to go

Publicly Mrs. Rodgers always dressed appropriately, in nylon stockings, a pillbox hat with netting secured with hat pins, sensible high-heeled shoes, white gloves, and a small purse that hung neatly from her wrist. Her curly hair—never seen down until bedtime—was always coiffed atop her head, the finishing touch being a pair of pearl earrings.

She managed "The Inn," a sandwich shop on the Talladega campus, seeing the need for a fast-food alternative for on-the-go students, all while shepherding her brood through Talladega. Dr. and Mrs. Rodgers bought the property directly adjacent to their home on 1618 Cooper and built multiple double-unit rental homes. 1616 Cooper became their son Gordon's dental practice, and now their granddaughter's. Through the years, my grandparents acquired a commercial building that housed an ice cream shop and multiple duplex housing units on Cooper Avenue (1616, 1612, 1610) used as rental properties or temporary housing for family. My grandfather hired a contractor to build their family home based on a conceptual sketch drawn on an envelope. My grandmother was unabashedly outspoken, courageous, and knew how to promote her ideas.

PROFESSIONAL LIFE OF DR. GORDON A. RODGERS

"Our father was an MD and pharmacist, which made a big difference in what you could do," said Gordon, Jr. "He owned a combination office and pharmacy—an advantageous pairing as there were no drugstores." Dr. Charles Thomas had operated a large pharmacy in Anniston since the 1800s without the benefit of a registered pharmacist to fill prescriptions. "My daddy heard about this opportunity and positioned himself to take the state pharmacy board following his sophomore year in medical school, as if he had attended pharmacy school."

Dr. Thomas hired Gordon Rodgers, Sr. following his pharmacy certification for two summers while attending medical school. Following medical school graduation in 1908, Gordon, Sr. opened his medical office.

Dr. Gordon Rodgers, Sr., 15th Street Drugstore Pharmacy

1923 DRUGSTORE OPENING /PARENTS

Gordon explained, "In 1923, my parents decided to open a drugstore/pharmacy on 15th Street; my mother was the businessperson/business head in the family." The drugstore was built and all supplies ordered when there was a sudden change of plans.

Dr. B, a Talladega doctor, drugstore owner, and family friend, became entangled with the Ku Klux Klan. Dr. B was eventually run out of town and forced to give up his drugstore on Battle Street, based on accusations of involvement with a white woman. Having learned this, Gordon, Sr. canceled the Birmingham orders and purchased supplies from Dr. B's drugstore. "He traveled to Talladega with a big truck, transported supplies to Anniston, and that marked the beginning of my daddy's drugstore."

The entire Rodgers family worked at the drugstore over time. Gordon, Jr. was the soda jerk. My father explained, "In the winter, my job was to bottle and label five-gallon containers of cough syrup and sell it for twenty-five cents. Nobody could pay you, and that's why I went into public health."

Thirty-seven years later, SUR would make use of this first-hand work experience. He would conceptualize then physically plan both the doctors' clinic of Kansas City and the Samuel U. Rodgers Community Health Center, based on the knowledge he gained in his father's pharmacy drugstore. He learned to be flexible and pivot as the times required. SUR was unknowingly being groomed for strategic vision, entrepreneurship, and leadership.

GENERAL JAMES (JIM) R. HALL, JR. INTERVIEW, OCTOBER 26, 2021
The phrase "big men come from small places" often comes to mind when I think about Anniston, Alabama, and the great men and women produced by this community. These achievers were, at their core, good and decent people. Jim Hall's parents grew up in Anniston with the three Rodgers siblings, Elouise, Gordon, Jr., and Samuel, but Hall remembered SUR's father the best.

Dr. Gordon Rodgers, Sr., the only African American Doctor in Calhoun County at the time, was not allowed to practice in the hospital. His drugstore, located on West 15th Street (between Steven and Brown Avenues), had over-the-counter medications. "Whenever you were sick you called Dr. Rodgers and he would make a house call unless you visited the drugstore. Dr. Rodgers never got rich because if you couldn't pay him, you paid him whatever you could—whenever you could."

Dr. Rodgers recommended what you needed, and people had confidence in his diagnosis. Jim didn't recall having another doctor in Anniston until 1951–52 during the polio outbreak. Doc Rodgers advised people of what to do and what not to do.

Jim's family were members of First Congregational Church (First Church) where the Rodgers family attended. Jim recalled Mrs. Rodgers' activism in the Missionary Society and Sunday school but didn't remember seeing Dr. Rodgers in church that often:

"Mrs. Rodgers was one of the leaders in our community and organized multiple efforts with the women's missionary. First Church, at the corner of 15th and Mulberry Streets, was located at a major bus stop with heavy foot traffic. Not everybody had a car and most men got paid on Friday afternoon and Saturday. Mrs. Rodgers organized a fish fry on this corner and the missionary women fried and sold fish dinners, well into the night. There were a lot of people walking down the street that day, and it paid off."

Jim would refer to my father as "Ulysses" throughout the interview, a middle name not used since my grandmother's death over fifty years ago. "Everybody called him Ulysses, even my parents. I thought Ulysses was his first name." My father would assume multiple names, throughout his lifetime: Ulysses, Sam, Butch, Uncle Pee-Wee, Daddy, and Doc.

Gordon, Jr. became the president of the NAACP, and my parents built a new home directly across the street from the Gordon Rodgers family. We were a close-knit group. If you needed help the answer was never no, but always yes. It was yes because of the love of the neighborhood and the closeness of the people there. Nothing was done for any kind of monetary compensation. "It was nice growing up in Anniston."

Jim's observation of my grandfather's church attendance was not a questionable recollection, but the truth. My church attendance with my father occurred at First Church in Anniston, during our summer visits. Our entire family attended in tow (including all three Dr. Rodgers) due to my grandmother's skills of persuasion, expectation, and persistence. More easily put, you simply didn't say no to her, and going along was much easier than not.

My grandfather and father were not quoters of scripture, nor frequent pew warmers. They understood the benefits of a foundational Christian upbringing as they had received. They both pivoted to a more activist hands-on "grass roots street ministry" where they believed the needs of the community could be more actively addressed. Given the status of health care in the African American community, there was no time to be lulled into a sense of complacency. Both men continued to be led by the Spirit within them. Now was the time to act.

Jim Crow South Education

TALLADEGA ALABAMA

Life was dangerous in the Jim Crow South where a person could be innocently charged, tried, and convicted, or worse, murdered within seconds of being approached by an unrepentant and unprosecuted white community. You could lose your job, business, reputation, and life because of your skin color.

I had come to understand that my granddaddy Gordon, Sr. lived a life of self-preservation out of necessity. No lawfully appointed police force or sheriff would arrive when called for *his* protection. He had to be prepared for his demise at their hands. I recall lying awake on hot summer nights at my grandparents' home. I could hear the ordered sound of my granddaddy's shuffling feet—in leather bound slippers—moving silently in the direction of his "safe" room in case of emergency, the locked room that contained his firearms, money, and our family's freedom and safety. My thoughts were confirmed as the Rodgers brothers continued with reflections of their father, Dr. Gordon A. Rodgers, Sr.

"My daddy carried a pistol all the time with a don't-bother-me mentality," said Gordon.

This interview revealed many things I had never known before. What I knew for sure was that my grandfather, a learned and gentle man, educated, loved, and protected his family, his most prized accomplishment and blessing. His life's options were unfortunately formed by the unlawful realities of the times, and things not of his choosing.

Gordon, Sr. was born into a world without lawful protection of the black family and instead with laws intentionally legislated for their destruction. On March 6, 1857, in the infamous Dred Scott decision, the US Supreme Court decided that African Americans "had no rights which the white man was bound to respect." (Columbian College of Arts & Sciences-The George Washington University/History News Network.)

Young Gordon A. Rodgers, Sr.

Throughout Gordon, Sr.'s lifetime (1884–1969), there were reportedly 340 victims of lynchings in Alabama. Ninety-three percent of the lynchings recorded occurred in his lifetime, several occurring in the counties/towns where he resided or frequented (Elmore County -Wetumpka, Calhoun County-Anniston, and the town of Talladega, Alabama.)

The National Memorial for Peace and Justice (Montgomery, Alabama), which memorializes the 4,400 lynchings of people in 800 counties from 1877 through 1950, was established across the street from Old Ship Zion AME Church, the church pastored by Gordon Sr.'s father; Rev. Alexander Joseph Rodgers. (More than 300 African Americans lynched in Alabama in 66 years, William Thornton)

TALLADEGA EDUCATION

The Rodgers siblings started school in Anniston but left home around the age of twelve. In Alabama following completion of grade school, black children were expected to work. "My daddy would say, so and so was going away to boarding school. It was a big deal," Gordon recalled.

The Rodgers boys were already living this reality vicariously through their older sister Elouise, attending Talladega College. Weese would return home for the Thanksgiving and Christmas holidays only. Talladega, Alabama, was a mere twenty-five miles away from Anniston, but too far to drive due to poor road conditions.

On May 17, 1954, the US Supreme Court declared state laws establishing separate public schools for students of different races to be unconstitutional. (Brown v. Board of Education of Topeka Kansas—US National Park Service /www: nps.gov)

By 1954 black people were no longer forced to leave home to complete a secondary education.

The Rodgers Siblings, their Mother
and several Talledega classmates

The interviewer asked, "And what kind of students were you?" Gordon, quick to reply with his trademark cat-that-ate-the-canary smile, said, "I really didn't give a damn." For the first time we all laughed out loud, interrupting the quiet of the library setting and fueling Uncle Gordon's mischievous streak. Samuel quickly remarked, "Because it was a private school, I knew I couldn't goof around because it didn't matter who your parents were."

Upon their arrival at Talladega, the brothers would be constantly reminded by their teachers of the brilliance and discipline of their sister Elouise and the good advice to follow her example as a model student.

The arrival of the three siblings marked the second generation of Rodgers to attend Talladega College; their mother Fannie was the first generation. Their mother would leave Anniston and her husband, Dr. Rodgers, behind to operate the pharmacy/medical practice, while she relocated to the small college town to monitor the studies and whereabouts of their three children.

My grandmother had attended Talladega, knew everybody there, and she and the children lived on campus in college housing. My father recalled the ambivalence of being students, while also living on campus like staff, with access to the gym, swimming pool, and college amenities.

My father didn't consider himself a bright student. He stated his goal was to do what he absolutely needed to do, not necessarily to produce grade-A quality work. "We had fun most of the time."

I was amused by my father's student self-revelations, noting what he would eventually accomplish on the world stage. Despite the brothers' nonchalance as young students, they progressed academically, aided by their mother's oversight. A mother knows her children, and Elouise needed no monitoring. My grandfather remained in Anniston attending to his medical practice and drugstore. All three siblings would complete their secondary and college educations (ages twelve through eighteen) on the Talladega campus that became their home away from home.

On March 2, 2022, after completion of this writing, I received new information from Elouise's daughter, Janet Ransom. I sat staring at a texted photo of a yellowed, wrinkled paper document. In calligraphy script it read, "Drewry Practice High School of Talladega College, Talladega, Alabama. This is to certify that Frances Elouise Rodgers has satisfactorily completed the prescribed studies of the Senior High School Course, and is hereby awarded this certificate—May 30, 1930."

1930 Drewry Practice High School Certificate

Talladega College Graduates:

- Frances Elouise Rodgers, 1935—Bachelor of Arts, education (cum laude)

- Gordon Alexander Rodgers, Jr., 1937—Bachelor of Science
- Samuel Ulysses Rodgers, 1937—Bachelor of Science

Samuel added, "I finished high school in 1933 (age fifteen), and college in 1937 (age eighteen). When I was ready to go to medical school—following college graduation—they said I was too young. I remained on the Talladega campus one more year after I graduated."

My father had officially completed his college studies at the age of eighteen, having skipped a level along the way, graduating from Talladega the same year as his older brother Gordon.

Young Samuel—Tuskegee Studio

Talladega offered more than a fine liberal arts education. Lifetime friendships were forged with other children who flocked to this institute from all parts of the US, many arriving in chauffeur-driven limousines and with stacks of luggage, as my father would recall. Elouise would eventually marry into the Ransom family, a schoolmate connection that began at Talladega. The Ransoms, a prominent family from the Midwest, were best known through patriarch Freeman Briley "FB" Ransom, a civic leader and Indianapolis businessman. I would learn that, most notably he became Madame CJ Walker's right-hand man and served as the attorney and general manager for the Madam CJ Walker manufacturing company. In 1939, FB Ransom became Elouise's father-in-law.

Francis Elouise will become Ransom bride

MIND, BODY, AND SPIRIT

Dr. and Mrs. Rodgers exercised parental discipline with their children, educating and protecting them emotionally and spiritually and building them up to believe in themselves, to know their value in an America that would institute and legislate against their humanity. The role of black parents is an enormously underestimated responsibility in a world that invests daily in the constant erosion of their soul and spirit. They have the honor yet the unenviable task of raising children to survive the unthinkable horrors. They—like so many other parents— had to build within their children what the world would soon tear down. These children needed self-confidence and to know their value early on to combat the racism that would confront them at every turn. The ability to survive the Jim Crow South was a foundational requirement; however, these parents had their eyes on a much bigger prize. They believed and expected their children to thrive and excel. Although young Ulysses was academically prepared, his parents held on just a little longer to allow his spirit and body to sync with his mind.

The Rodgers family

The Talladega College commitment was certainly in keeping with my grandparents' philosophy. Education was the key to freedom and vital to the preservation of African American liberties. (Talladega College-Our College /www: <u>Talladega.</u> <u>edu</u>)

The Rodgers Talladega family migration was my father's first example of the importance of education and of the parental and self-sacrifice often required to be educated. He would make a similar decision roughly forty years later to temporarily separate from his immediate family to achieve a much bigger educational goal.

Gordon finished dental school in 1941 and Samuel completed medical school in 1942. Though outwardly different in personality—the brothers shared a carefree nonchalance that would shield them under fire, the incinerating fire they would both face in the dismantling of racist institutions in the cities where they made their livelihoods. (The Forgotten History of Defunct Medical Schools in the 19th and 20th Centuries and the Impact of the Flexner Report—Earl H. Harley, MD. (NIH National Library of Medicine. PMC PubMed Central—Journal of the National Medical Association, Sept. 2006, Earl H. Harley.)

The brothers would part for the first time to attend different dental and medical schools. When questioned about this they paused, then responded simultaneously, "By that time we'd had enough of each other." Their candid confession would produce the second loudest round of laughter that day.

Dr. Samuel U. Rodgers, Howard Medical School graduate

After our group regained composure, the next question revealed my father's heartfelt dreams and pending dilemmas. "After medical school, did you go to Kansas City?" Reflecting momentarily, my father inhaled and slowly responded, "WW2 came, and I landed in Kansas City, Missouri—the step between medical school and deciding what I wanted to be. I decided to be a surgeon, but the dilemma was where would I be trained?"

SUR WORLD WAR II EXPERIENCE

"During WWII there was no black doctor in a hospital at *any level* doing major operations, or an *example* of a black surgeon. Black people did not have the opportunity to receive postgraduate specialty training after medical school. You could not possibly become a surgeon without specialty training," my father explained.

Following completion of medical school, my father enlisted in the army as a doctor. For blacks in the US, the missing link was specialty training that ideally should follow completion of medical school. A military center existed at Fort Huachuca, but they were unable to find enough trained physicians to operate a program.

As I listened to my father recount this difficult chapter of his life, I was stuck between frustration and disbelief knowing how the story ended. My reliving of his pain was paralyzing. My father would become a member of the Ninety-second Infantry Division's Medical Battalion of the Buffalo Soldiers, stationed in Italy. My frustration slowly melted to pride.

"I was in charge of fifteen to twenty ambulances, responsible for picking up injured soldiers and getting them to medical care," he said.

Gordon Rodgers was a dentist in the same division, where the brothers met frequently in various parts of Italy.

No whole blood transfusions existed in the beginning of World War II; only blood plasma was available. "White people didn't want to receive blood from black people, creating a major issue eventually involving Mrs. Eleanor Roosevelt," my father incredulously said. Smiling knowingly, he said, "The injured men dying on the field could care less whether the blood they received was from black or white people."

Until the end of WWII, the US had two distinct armies based on race: one black and the other white. The war ended, still without specialty training programs for black physicians. Unearthing decades-old frustrations, he captured in few words the defining dilemma of his life. You could not become a qualified surgeon without the required training. There were no training sites for black physicians, nor trained personnel willing or able to teach them. President Harry S. Truman signed Executive Order 9981 on July 26, 1948, ending segregation in the US military.

In 1955, my father met President Truman who would play a major role in making my father's yet unrealized dream come true (Farrell Evans, Nov 5, 2020).

FAMILY LIFE IN KANSAS CITY, MISSOURI, 1963

In my childhood home in Kansas City, my father kept his most cherished memories of World War II in his wood-paneled den, his quiet room. He had a heavy, lockable metal box where he stored dozens of small Kodak slides and black-and-white photographs taken during his tour of duty in Italy. It was stored in a built-in wall cabinet that also housed his collection of classical music, and books.

He was a lover of art, music, literature, and travel. Occasionally, we sat together in the den where he would revisit his army days, sharing stories with my brother, sister, and me in our elementary school years. Our father spoke of training in Fort Huachuca, Arizona, and of traveling across the Italian countryside. There were photographs of the Italian countryside, the town of Viareggio, fellow gun-toting soldiers, and army tanks. There was—unforgettably—a black-and-white photograph of a town square, in Milan, Italy. My father had been there at the Piazzale Loreto Square—an eyewitness to the fateful ending place of Benito Mussolini, first executed then hung upside down in the town square. (The National WWII Museum, "Death of Duce, Benito Mussolini" Website)

What my father explained then was the horrifying picture and the ravages of war that verified this historic account. My parents and grandparents never shielded us in childhood from the harsh reality of our lives as African Americans. No issue was sugarcoated or dressed up to be anything other than the "age-appropriate" truth.

However, the most cherished—and visibly prominent—of all WWII mementos was the one that hung on the brick wall above the fireplace in the den. It was a massive wood carving of an Italian countryside that was approximately six feet wide and four feet high and at least four inches deep. Running my hands across the face of the mural I could feel and see the three-dimensional qualities and trace around the carved trees and houses. The mural was found near the end of WWII, as his medical battalion traveled through a bombed-out village. The mural was one of the few items that remained intact in this Jewish family's home; a family most likely forcibly removed by the German army and their collaborators during the Holocaust.

I will never know how he managed to transport the mural across Italy and back to the US. When he ran into brick walls—like Superman—he miraculously appeared safely on the other side. What I knew for sure was that my father was not a quitter but an overcomer.

SUR POST-WORLD WAR II, 1945

Deeply engrossed in SUR's journey thus far, the interviewer asked, "You chose not to go back to Anniston?" SUR responded, "I did return to Anniston right out of the army. My father and I planned to practice together—our life-long dream. But I couldn't be on the white staff at the Anniston hospital, not as a specialist or anything else. My daddy had contended with years of racism and discrimination. He eventually commanded, 'Get out of Anniston and go somewhere you can practice.'"

"A turning point in our lives, my father was visibly upset by this miscarried dream to practice with his son. My father, Gordon Sr., made up his mind that if he ever got sick, he would never seek treatment at an Anniston hospital. During our 1961 Anniston summer visit, he suffered a massive heart attack and flatly refused to seek medical care at the hospital. A doctor was summoned, he remained at home, self-prescribed, and lived another eight to ten years."

Gordon added, "I returned to Anniston, and my mother told me that she had a place picked out for me, and I stayed there. It was a complicated time." The brothers were separated once again.

Dr. Gordon Alexander Rodgers, Sr., the first generation born free in 1884, subjected to the disparaging rules of the Jim Crow South, had seen more than enough. His life had proven that he would not and could not trust nor depend on the white establishment to mete out justice fairly. He became his own home-based hospital, pharmacy/drugstore, bank, and safety/police force. After eighty-five years of living, he knew the score.

His obituary read, "Dr. Gordon A. Rodgers, Sr. of 1618 Cooper Avenue died at his home, Sunday morning, August 31, 1969. Death came suddenly." His early educational training was received at the State Normal School in Montgomery, Alabama. He received a medical degree from Meharry College in 1908. Dr. Rodgers practiced medicine in Anniston, Alabama, until his death. Dr. Rodgers was active in civic and community affairs. He was a life longtime Scout committee man and was a recipient of the District Scouters Award. Other honors include his citation for outstanding work during World Wars I and II. He was awarded the Selective Service Medal and a certificate of appreciation from the President of the United States for twenty-five years of service. He received a plaque for being a lifetime member of NAACP.

STAND

My sister blogged years later as a Memorial Day Tribute: "My father, a Major in the segregated Army Medical Corps, WWII, was barred by the white medical establishment upon his return to Anniston after rescuing many white soldiers on the battlefields of Italy. When he returned to Alabama to practice with his father, he could not get hospital privileges, so my grandfather told him to get as far from Alabama as he could. I was told that this shattered dream broke my grandfather's heart. But he resolved that the limits of racism and segregation would not impede the legacy." ("Dr. Rodgers Historical/Family History." Black History Month Rodgers Family blog. August 9, 2018. Facebook)

Dr. Samuel Rodgers fought for justice at home and in Europe. He served in the military from 1943 to 1946 with the Ninety-second Infantry Division in Italy, first as platoon commander then as company commander in the 317 Medical Battalion, receiving the Combat Medical Badge. He returned home hopeful for his future, having won the freedoms for others that he would never meet. Upon his return to the United States, having proven his valor, he like many African American soldiers faced resentment, violence from whites who resented seeing black soldiers in uniform, and often denial of benefits guaranteed under the G.I. Bill.

What does it take to carry out your dreams? And once accomplished, what does it take to keep dreaming? Dr. Rodgers' dream was about to come true. If African Americans sat down every time they faced discriminatory barriers, they would never stand up again.

MIDWEST
MIGRATION
(1942–1950)

Going to Kansas City

"Start by doing what's necessary, then do what's possible; and suddenly you are doing the impossible."

—FRANCES OF ASSISI

I imagine the voice of our ancestors speaking to my father:

"Should disappointments over shattered dreams signal the end of a heartfelt quest? No, reorient yourself and continue to seek the same North Star of your ancestors. For our enslaved ancestors the North Star was a sign of freedom, with the journey's end untold. Follow it to secure education—the new freedom although what you can accomplish is yet unknown. Follow and lead as your ancestors did before."

THE 1942 KANSAS CITY MIGRATION

For SUR the move to Kansas City represented another "migration moment" in his life. He moved from Anniston to Talladega, Alabama at age ten: then from Talladega to Washington, DC, to attain a medical degree—all for the hope of gaining an education. The value of this latest migration was yet to be appreciated.

"Go. There is nothing here for you," were Gordon, Sr.'s parting words of wisdom to his son.

I try to imagine my father's gut reaction at hearing his own father's most disappointing words, following years of educational preparation and dreams. The underlying message was, "Go and make a way for yourself, somewhere else; our dream can't and won't happen here." What searing words to process, the words you never thought you would hear but needed to acknowledge in that moment. This was a father's love.

SUR wanted most of all to become a qualified surgeon, which required specialized training. He set his eyes, heart, and mind on this goal. In WWII he had served as company commander in the 317 Medical Battalion, receiving the Combat Medical Badge. He needed to figure out the next step in his journey, knowing the what but not the how.

His lifelong dream was not only to become a surgeon, but to return to his hometown of Anniston following WWII to practice medicine with Dr. Gordon A. Rodgers, Sr., his father and mentor. His brother Gordon received an honorable discharge from the army in 1944 with the rank of Captain and returned home as well to begin his private practice in dentistry. It was to be an African American health care dynasty: a father and two sons. A family who wanted to serve their community that had given so much to them.

Unfortunately, this dream would not manifest in the city of Anniston. It was not possible because of the systemic racism of the Jim Crow South, prevalent even in the field of medicine. A system that would not offer specialty training sites for black physicians to become surgeons. My father had by now lived a lifetime of less-than-perfect options as belief systems, laws, and people can hold you captive.

Reliving his frustration, my father said, "It was a vicious cycle to apply for training only to be told, 'We don't train black physicians in medical specialties,' and without specialty training I could only be a generalist. My first move when I returned to the United States was to try to do something about that system," recalled my father in a 1998 interview with family.

My father attended Howard Medical School (1938–1942) before WWII when there were no approved surgical programs. He returned from WWII in search of this training, determined to attack the system head on.

The returning doctors and military vets remained angry and vowed to create opportunities in specialty training.

My father was an ace at understanding issues, coupled with the courage to implement a boat rocking plan.

There were only two black universities where this was remotely possible, each with inherent limitations. Howard University had Charles Drew, yet not enough certified black MDs to train medical students and no approved three-year OB-GYN training service. The system was fixed to promote stalemates with problems at every level. "The system was not solving these two requirements, and that was the crisis," SUR said.

In 1942, Kansas City had one of only three or four major hospitals in the United States staffed by black people. Many black doctors rotated through either Kansas City, St. Louis, Missouri, or Chicago, Illinois, to staff these black hospitals.

"Kansas City built a brand-new, but segregated, hospital facility. It was a unique situation that presented unique opportunities," he explained. Yet, who would be willing to teach black physicians there? There were no existing black physician role models who could help.

"There were fair and sensible white people in this country who understood the problem."

Howard University Medical School representatives traveled to New Haven, Connecticut, to make a financial transaction with the surgical department. The transaction ensured the hiring and relocation of a white surgeon to Howard to start a training program that would provide the first opportunity for black doctors to attain the level of eligibility required to be considered a trained surgeon. This was the turning point that triggered the change.

THE MIDWEST MIGRATION:
OB-GYN SPECIALTY/INTERNSHIP, 1942–1943

In 1942, following graduation from Howard Medical School, SUR moved to Kansas City, Missouri, armed with a medical degree and a big dream to receive specialty training—seemingly with no solution in sight.

This specialty training was most certainly the missing link. SUR was twenty-five years old, hopeful, determined, and courageous. He was, most importantly, already clothed in the essential family values of integrity, morality, and honesty, learned from the example and actions taken by his grandfather and father when they were confronted with adversity and uncertainty. He was ahead of his time in thought process and wisdom, with an emotional maturity that would serve his future purposes well. Although the dream would not manifest where originally thought, could his dream of becoming a surgeon still come true?

General Hospital No. 2 (GH2), the segregated black hospital, was staffed by black nurses and physicians and presented a unique opportunity. Relocation to a new city is also more bearable if you are accompanied by a local native Kansas Citian.

KANSAS CITY MOMENTS: 1942

UP TO THE TASK

My father showed a rare ability throughout his life of easily balancing addressing personal as well as professional issues at once. He excelled at multitasking, decades before the term became overused. He could compartmentalize, putting certain tasks on hold while going full steam ahead on others, prioritizing and scheduling all complex issues he was addressing on the same plate. Years later I would recognize that when my father returned home at the end of the day, he removed his "Superman" cape worn daily in his uphill quest to transform health care delivery. When asked, "What would you like for dinner?" he would chuckle and say, "I think I've made enough decisions for today. I'll leave this one for someone else."

When he arrived in Kansas City in 1942 to begin his internship there was more to say grace over than even he imagined. At the same time, he was a young handsome, single twenty-five-year-old, wishing to have it all someday—a career and a loving family, just like the one that raised him.

MARRIAGE, FRIENDS, AND BROTHERS: 1944

My father had the distinct advantage of being safely ushered into this new city environment by a trusted friend who knew the ropes, Dr. Merle Hereford. Merle Hereford, newly graduated and armed with his medical degree, returned to Kansas City, his hometown. My father, unable to return to his hometown or gain hospital privileges, would adopt Kansas City as his own. Indeed, this Kansas City lifestyle was a major departure from Anniston, Alabama, and GH1 and GH2 stood on Hospital Hill just blocks away from the jazz district.

My father first met Merle at Howard Medical School where they toiled together to complete their educations as expected by their families. They became fast friends and comrades during this critically developmental phase of their lives: their early '20s.

"That Merle is just a brilliant guy," my father would continue to say for years, with a smile of awe. As a child I thought of him as an African American Einstein; he was kind, quick, and witty in a subtle way. My father came to know many people throughout his life, but Dr. Merle Hereford was indeed my father's best friend.

Merle, as my father would come to learn, was much aligned with my father's low-key personality and steady nature. They adopted each other as brothers and followed each other to new opportunities in Kansas City. They were both seriously intent about self-responsibility, family, and contributing to their community.

Recognizing the importance of relaxation, they set out one evening to unwind between their stress-filled patient rounds as interns at GH2. My father's brother Gordon also pursued one of the few options for black interns and serendipitously ended up at GH2 around the same time. Soon after the

Rodgers brothers arrived in Kansas City, Merle suggested an evening out with old friends.

Merle Hereford grew up on West Paseo, one block away from the Pullam family home located on the corner of 24th Street and Paseo Boulevard. The Hereford and Pullam families had known each other all their lives. From atop West Paseo you could look downhill and across the park and spot the two-story stone-and-brick home of the Pullams with the metaphoric revolving front door. The Pullam household, headed by Mr. Arthur Eugene "Chick" Pullam, a career postal worker, was a popular place.

The Pullams were a well-known, respected, and beloved family in the black community, having established a family reputation of achievement. They were a warm, loving family. Arthur and Beulah Pullam had successfully raised four daughters, Alma, Willa, Elizabeth, and Barbara, and two sons, Arthur, Jr. and Richard, all who graduated college from either Lincoln University in Jefferson City, Missouri or the University of Kansas in Lawrence, Kansas. Chick Pullam's older brother, Bill Houston (alias "Uncle Bill"), graduated from the segregated, all-white University of Kansas with a degree in pharmacy in the late 1800s with no discovery by school officials of his African American descent.

The evening was arranged, and sisters Elizabeth and Barbara, high school classmates and neighbors of Merle, looked forward to meeting his new friends. The sisters trusted Merle like a brother and readily agreed to what could be nothing less than a fun evening. SUR trusted Merle as a brother too and may have wondered about the real purpose of the outing. The three young interns never had enough time to sleep, much less go out on the town.

Neither Merle nor SUR were risk-takers so this assumed that Merle's evening venture would land on a very positive note. I imagine they may have met in or around the 18th and Vine District, where most young people would spend a night out. It was a pseudo-blind date with a pair of two sisters and two brothers who had never met each other, and a single friend who knew them all very well.

At the evening's end, without knowing Dr. Hereford's intended plan, my father was clearly interested in the older of the two sisters, whom he would come to call Liz.

Young Elizabeth Jane Pullam

ELIZABETH JANE PULLAM

My mother grew up in the heart of the negro community, as it was considered at the time. She attended Lincoln High School (LHS), the only school available to African Americans. Lincoln sat atop a hill just blocks away, overlooking this active jazz hamlet that continues to hold such history. She grew up in a protected, segregated, and thriving community on Paseo Boulevard, several blocks from the now infamous "12th Street and Vine."

My mother's family and closest friends called her Lizzie. She was refreshing and vivacious without being annoying. My mother was not fussy, materialistic, or full of herself. She had the ability to see through people's façades and often their self-imposed issues. Momma was visionary, as was Daddy, but in a much more cerebral way. She was politely no nonsense and could see through foolishness as easily as one could see through a window. More importantly she could see into the hearts of people, and other people could see her true heart as well. She was authentic and genuinely kind. Elizabeth Pullam was a "Lena Horne" beauty, without the air or edge of some beautiful women. She was beautiful inside and out and became the confidant of many whose secrets she took to her grave—always trustworthy, steady, low-key, and unfrazzled, just like my dad.

In April of 1944, my parents were married at my mother's childhood home on 2427 Paseo Boulevard. With little notice, my father was asked to report back to his WWII post within days. SUR was beginning his military service period of 1943 to 1946. It was a quickly planned ceremony, and they married in my grandparents' front parlor with no fanfare. My mother was dressed beautifully in a nicely appointed suit, my father in his captain's uniform as he had no ready access to a nice suit. I concluded that Dr. Merle Hereford was indeed a genius for his match-making skills. My parents were a match made in heaven.

Years later, as I looked at the old wedding pictures of the newlyweds posed before the parlor fireplace, I was reminded of family stories and the earlier significance of this parlor many decades before. During my mother's infant years, her parents, like many, experienced loss and hardship. The eldest Pullam sibling Alma's funeral visitation was held in this parlor, as was common in homes of that time. My mother married in the parlor with passed-down memories of her eldest sister Alma, whom she never knew. Big sister Alma died at the age of eight from a ruptured appendix, as she fell on the sidewalk while roller skating in front of the Pullam home. I wondered what level of medical care was accessible to this black community at that time. My father's mission to integrate the segregated hospitals for improved health care was decades overdue.

My parents met during his internship at GH2, and my father would understandably describe my mother in less than romantic, clinical lingo. "She was an intern's dream!" he loved to exclaim. My father was referencing my mother's small build, thin arms, and virtually transparent skin that easily showed every blood vessel in her arm, providing an obvious road map for any new intern.

Clinical or not, these are the words and story I repeat at every doctor's appointment, as I prepare for a blood draw. I share my father's story with every technician, and as I roll up my sleeve they laugh and understand why.

Although my father was confronted with new racial challenges in Kansas City, he received many new blessings. He learned to find a silver lining in every cloud, a priceless lesson that would serve him well in the coming years.

General Hospital No. 2

HISTORIC WRITINGS JOURNEY AND TRIBUTE

I have always known my father was a planner, a visionary, a strategist. The amazement was that I took it for granted and thought most people were like this. These things had just become a part of my normal world. I was not aware, until after his death, that he was also an author and prolific storyteller.

Old building, Kansas City General Hospital No. 2.

Old building, Kansas City General Hospital No. 2

In preparation for the Fiftieth Anniversary Gala celebration event, I found an article written by SUR in the September

1962 Journal of the National Medical Association entitled "Original Communications—Kansas City General Hospital No. 2; A Historical Summary." I wondered if he had planted these seeds of history to be discovered serendipitously as they were. I'm convinced he documented this story as a roadmap for whomever would need these lessons again someday. History has a way of repeating itself.

SUR was a quiet and unassuming person, unless and until some person or practice stood in the way of making progress for a community of people who remained medically underserved. Many people and institutions through the years found themselves on the other side of this mission, an uncomfortable place to be with SUR. I knew certain stories passed down through his daily conversations, but never was I aware of this series of writings. Though appreciative of this article, I missed the opportunity to hear of these past victories in detail from my father. It is through this series of writings that I have come to know in more candid terms the heart of my father as a visionary.

SUR arrived in Kansas City in 1942. He served his internship in Kansas City General Hospital (GH2) from 1942 to 1943. SUR served as a major in the Medical Corps of the United States Army in World War II. He returned to GH2 for his residency training in OB-GYN from 1947 to 1950.

The condition for physicians in Kansas City at the time were far from ideal, especially for a young doctor seeking residency training. In an article published in JNMA September 1962, SUR noted the conditions in the Kansas City medical community when he arrived. Paraphrasing an April 1946 report by health specialist W. Montaque Cobb, MD, SUR said the following regarding professional race relations:

"*Racial separation continued and was perpetuated by both Negroes and whites concerning the health problems in Kansas City. Negroes viewed the situation as damnable but inevitable. The whites viewed separation as a preferable condition. The Negroes reacted with fuming resentment, or guardedly expressed their suppressed frustration. The condition allowed a simplistic display of patronizing condescension by influential whites, who chose to ignore the complexities of racial separation. All this is bad.*"

In regard to the condition of the Negro physician generally, SUR noted:

"*At present none of the Negro physicians have become certified specialists in any field. although size of population and hospital needs would lead to the anticipation of at least one in each field. Principal deterrents to the development of specialists have been the belief that the Negro community was too poor to support them and the fear on the part of men who would not be referred enough work. It was reported to the writer that one man attempted unsuccessfully to practice a specialty in a field commonly remunerative to the general practitioner and that the assembled Negro physicians had seriously considered the advisability of welcoming any new colleagues because of the belief that the present number of physicians was the saturation point for the economic level of the community.*"

Finally, as for conditions at GH2 at the time, SUR comments:

"*The hospital organization listed eighteen services. The heads of services are not certified specialists in the respective fields, except in the case of certain white physicians whose major responsibilities are elsewhere. The organization of the staff is too informal; responsibility is not adequately fixed, and satisfactory coverage is not assured. The majority of physicians in senior positions have not had the training or specialized practice, which they should obtain for such positions in a major institution. Staff meetings tend to be poorly attended and the material of clinical conferences not developed to desirable potentialities. Two major services, pathology and radiology were without the active supervision of proper specialists. Under such arrangements interns cannot receive adequate training nor patients the best care. Unfortunate historical circumstances have not gained for the hospital a reputation which would place a premium on its internships."*

DOUBLE-EDGED DILEMMA

SUR faced a double-edged dilemma. The assessment was candid and thorough. There was no doubt that quantifiable conditions inhibited patient care and the training of black physicians that would care for black patients. The lack of available training for black physicians, a result of systemic racism, reflected external forces at work. Internally, many black physicians were plagued by self-doubt, an underestimation of community needs, and of their personal strength to right the wrong. Both conditions resulted from centuries of racial discrimination, the most damaging of which was the effect of discrimination on the human spirit. Given these conditions, not only did my father face the Jim Crow South normalization of the black existence, but he also had to combat the beliefs of some entrenched black physicians. Old habits die hard, and years of insult had been internalized;

many black souls had withered in defeat. There was indifference on both sides, white and black.

The report showed that efforts had been made, with varying degrees of success. Doctors were sometimes trained in their chosen fields by outstanding men until they qualified as certified specialists—and then what? By other examples, excellent opportunities for advanced training and development opened to individual black physicians but had not turned out well.

I slowed down and re-read the descriptions of the seemingly immovable conditions, wondering what my father had thought. Was this more than he bargained for, or was this to become his David and Goliath opportunity? The report said, "there had been individuals of vision and good will" who had attempted to right these wrongs; but given the status as outlined in the report, the actions taken were to no avail.

As I continued reading, the stakes became increasingly more dire. I can only picture my father in the face of all these obstacles of the times, some expected and some undercover surprises.

These thoughts transported me back to the family room of our home in Kansas City. As a child I would see my father sitting quietly at the table in our family room that faced west. The entire extent of the west elevation, formed by sliding glass doors, provided an uninterrupted view of the park in the distance. He would sit staring westerly in deep thought, periodically glancing down at a medical journal in his lap. Growing up in that house, I had no idea of the gravity of issues he had faced and overcome. I never saw my father flinch. He was as cool as they come. He would sit with his one leg crossed, right ankle resting atop his left knee, occasionally toying with his mustache as he pondered his next challenge and the worries of the world. He would often say, "Rocky [my nickname), don't sweat the small stuff," and to him it was all small enough to correct.

Hospital Hill Desegregation

THE STRATEGIC POINT

By 1946, my father had received a WWII Combat Medical Badge in the segregated Medical Corps of the US Army, Ninety-second Infantry Division. He'd fought valiantly for the rights of Europeans, only to return to his native land with few civil rights. As an American he dutifully served his country. As an African American his country chose not to serve him. He was denied specialty training and ultimately the personal freedom to return home to practice medicine. Even so, SUR was hopeful, courageous, and determined. He was primed for change, as he walked through the history making doors of General Hospital No. 2.

In 1946, my father would author a comprehensive history of the conditions of General Hospitals No. 1 and No. 2. (J.N.M.A. Vol. 54, No.5, "Kansas City General Hospital No. 2: 1946")

JOURNAL OF THE NATIONAL MEDICAL ASSOCIATION
September, 1962 · Vol. 54 · No. 5

KANSAS CITY GENERAL HOSPITAL NO. 2

A Historical Summary

SAMUEL U. RODGERS, M.D.

Kansas City General Hospital and the Doctors Clinic,
Kansas City, Missouri

EDITOR'S NOTE: Kansas City General Hospital No. 2 ceased to exist in November 1957, as Dr. Rodgers describes, when Kansas City General Hospital No. 1 for whites and No. 2 for Negroes were ordered consolidated and existing plant and facilities reorganized accordingly. In order to present as current a picture as possible Dr. Rodgers has supplemented his story with descriptions of integration developments in other hospitals and other medical areas in Kansas City. In this he has had the assistance of Sister Madeline Marie, who wrote the section on Queen of the World Hospital, Dr. James S. Johnson, who wrote the section on the Kansas City Medical Society and Drs. W. R. Peterson and W. F. Haith, who wrote the section on group practice in Kansas City. The *Journal* is deeply indebted to Dr. Rodgers and his associates for the very comprehensive job they have done. The *Journal* also takes grateful notice of the individuals mentioned by Dr. Rodgers in his personal acknowledgements and particularly Dr. Lon M. Tillman. The *Journal* is also deeply indebted to Dr. Rodgers for collating the manuscripts from Kansas City authors and to the authors themselves. In addition, because of personal knowledge of developments, the editor would like to salute with appreciation the many individuals and groups who have worked long and patiently to bring about the changes of recent years.

AT the turn of the century, public hospitalization for Kansas City, Missouri, non-white population was very limited. There existed on Holmes Street, overlooking the Belt railroad tracks, the Kansas City Municipal Hospital, later to become known as "Old City Hospital." This structure built in about 1873, with some later additions, housed for 35 years the indigent sick whites, with a few beds for the non-whites (Negro and Mexican).

In June 1903 Kansas City was devastated by a flood, the worst on record up to that time. This emergency found the health and sanitation facilities totally inadequate, at least in regards to Negro victims of the flood. Convention Hall, a large auditorium, was pressed into service for use as a hospital primarily for these flood suffers. Selected to administer medical care to this group was a well known Negro doctor named Thomas C. Unthank. While serving in this capacity he conceived the idea of a City hospital for the training of young Negro men and women in the fine arts and science of the profession of medicine and nursing.

Thomas C. Unthank, in addition to being a good doctor, was a shrewd politician and a better than

DR. THOMAS C. UNTHANK

In 1946, General Hospital No. 2 (GH2) was selected as the strategic point to begin bringing medical care to its highest possible standards. GH2 was now approved by the American College of Surgeons for interns but not for residents. General Hospital No. 1, the whites-only hospital, was approved for the training of both interns and residents. The Kansas City Survey of the National Urban League summarized that GH2 should be promptly qualified for approved residents and that this would require two things: (1) staff reorganization involving visiting staff headed by certified specialists and (2) the cooperation of Negro physicians.

"As there are no specialists among the thirty-two Negro physicians in Kansas City, and as care of the patient must come before racial consideration, the cooperation of the Negro would be essential to ensure the success of any changes."

The conditions to be addressed were presented during meetings with both the Kansas City Medical Society (white physicians) and the local Negro medical association. It was unanimously agreed that the identified changes would require the support of the director of health and white physicians. The facts set forth in the conditions report represented, for some, the first objective critical analysis of the General Hospital problem by competent authorities.

As human nature would predict, however, these same facts were met with extreme reaction, from total agreement to absolute denial, on both sides.

As a result, "Corrective action was not forthcoming from any of the parties involved in the management of the hospital."

A NEW DAY, 1947
Serendipitously, around the time of the stalemate, several former General Hospital interns, now WWII veterans in search of post-graduate medical training, returned to GH2. This group of veterans included my father, the courageous soon-to-be trailblazer, Dr. Samuel U. Rodgers.

It was at once clear to these veterans, my father among them, the standard of medical care was not what it should be. Several more conferences, were held between the house staff (black), the visiting staff (white), and the city health department.

However, as reported in the journal, "These meetings brought forth nothing of benefit and created a great deal of ill feeling between the house staff and the greater portion of the visiting staff." (J.N.M.A. Vol. 54, No.5—Kansas City General Hospital No. 2, 1946)

The house staff of GH2 (my father and colleagues) determined they would take action.

MAJOR ACCOMPLISHMENTS:

CITY HOSPITAL STRIKE

At the beginning of the twentieth century approximately twenty-two newspapers were published by Kansas City's African American community. By 1943, only one survived, and that was *The Kansas City Call*. *The Call*, as commonly referred by residents, was the trusted mouthpiece of the community and grew to become one of the most successful black newspapers in the nation.

On January 31, 1947, *The Call* broke the story about the determined action of the black staff of GH2. The newspaper headlines read, "City Hospital Doctors Strike." "House Staff Physicians and Interns at GH2 yesterday began an organized protest against the lack of sufficient and appropriate medical equipment and supplies, against the shortage of hospital staff and against poor administration at the hospital."

The physicians first announced their intentions to "curtail their activities until these conditions are remedied." Following the announcement, the physicians "barred a shocking array of substandard conditions at the institution," the details of which were unreported. The doctors were careful to also announce that patients would not suffer because of the protest, but that the protest was purposed to "inform the tax paying public of the evil conditions of the hospital."

MISSION ACCOMPLISHED, 1948 REBIRTH

The strike started by these young determined and courageous black physicians marked a new beginning. The wisdom of the strike was no longer questioned, and their actions marked the historic beginning of a different GH2. Within months, it was reported the hospital was well on its way toward qualifications as an American Medical Association-approved teaching hospital for interns and residents in certain specialties.

Dr. Harold L. Gainey, then a major department head in obstetrics-gynecology, would become a most special influence, friend, and mentor to my father. Seven years later (March 6, 1955), Dr. Gainey played a very special role in my life, delivering me into this world!

"Within a few years General Hospital No. 2 was fully approved for residency specialty training in radiology, obstetrics-gynecology, and general surgery." As complete cooperation was slow in achieving between the local medical society and all areas of the health department, GH2 produced a low but steady flow of well-trained graduates. The 1962 *JNMA* reported "fifteen board certified specialists now practicing across the U.S.A. had received their specialty training at GH2 since 1947." (J.N.M.A. journal, September 1962 pg. 534) My father was listed as well as fifteen other certified physicians, some of whom would become his future partners in a joint practice they would soon forge.

THE DOCTORS' CLINIC, 1949

In volume fifty-four of the 1962 *JNMA* the authors noted there had been a steady increase in the number of doctors entering medical groups. The types of group practice options and the pros and cons of group practice were weighed and presented. Doctors Peterson and Haith explained the clinic was set up as a "private multi-specialty" type with much consideration.

The authors wrote, "It was organized in 1949 by four young physicians whose philosophy was group practice of medicine and due to local circumstances prevalent at the time, suggested that an amalgamation of talents and efforts might prove beneficial. This was the first Negro group in the country, and as far as we know, it remains the only true Negro group practice of this kind."

"At the present time (1962) six physicians are all certified by a specialty board, or are board eligible":

- Walter R. Peterson, general surgery
- Carl M. Peterson, general surgery

- Samuel U. Rodgers, obstetrics-gynecology
- Starks J. Williams, pediatrics
- Walter F. Haith, obstetrics-gynecology
- Curtis U. Franklin, Jr., internal medicine

After reading this report, I was not surprised to find in the formation of their private practice that my father and his co-founding group of physician colleagues deliberated and recognized the significance of overarching factors (i.e., number of doctors, ages, specialties, relationship to the community medical picture) and just as critical, the personal characteristics (i.e., temperament, philosophy) most likely to result in well-rounded partnership success.

This amazing group of comrades and medical professionals had solved the riddle of partnership success. As Haith and Peterson would note in their report, "In most cases the failure of group practice occurs as a result of improper choice of participants, poor business acumen, and distribution of income. We believe that all of these causes can be alleviated with the application of one encompassing phase—a proper and solid foundation built on faith, cooperation, efficiency and enlightenment in the beginning." (J.N.M.A. journal, Vol. 54, No. 5, September 1962 pg. 542-543 / Authors; W.R. Peterson / W. F. Haith)

THE CLOSING OF KANSAS CITY GENERAL HOSPITAL NO. 2, 1957

The *JNMA* editor's note read: "Kansas City General Hospital No. 2 ceased to exist in November 1957, as Dr. Rodgers describes, when Kansas City General Hospital No. 1 for whites and No. 2 for Negroes were ordered consolidated and existing plant and facilities reorganized accordingly."

The editor goes on to explain that Dr. Rodgers supplemented his story with descriptions of integration developments in other hospitals and areas of medicine in Kansas City. In this effort to broaden the study my father invited other individuals to author portions of this historical summary.

"The Journal is deeply indebted to Dr. Rodgers and his associates for the very comprehensive job they have done. The Journal is also deeply indebted to Dr. Rodgers for collating the manuscripts from Kansas City authors themselves. In addition, because of personal knowledge of developments, the editor would like to salute with appreciation the many individuals and groups who have worked long and patiently to bring about the changes of recent years."

HOSPITAL HILL DESEGREGATION

The historical summary report ended with a list of accomplishments of each of the Kansas City General Hospital No. 2 authors in the issue, along with headshots of each.

I was not surprised in the least that he would honor his colleagues first by recruiting their efforts, then including their writings, and lastly paying tribute to everyone's accomplishments. Professional headshots were included of each author. His vision was inclusive, boast-less, and respectful of all people. My father summarized his own achievements to date as follows:

"Dr. Samuel U. Rodgers was born in Anniston, Alabama in 1917. He received the A.B. from Talladega College in 1937 and the M. D. from Howard University in 1942. The year 1942-43 served his internship in Kansas City General Hospital and from 1947-50 was a resident in obstetrics and gynecology in the same hospital. Dr. Rodgers was a major in the Medical Corps of the United State Army in World War II. He is a diplomate of the National Board of Medical Examiners and was certified by the American Board of Obstetrics and Gynecology in 1954 and is a fellow of the American College of Obstetrics and Gynecology. He is on the attending staff of Kansas City General Hospital and an associate in obstetrics and gynecology at the University Medical Center." (J.N.M.A. journal, Vol. 54, No. 5, September 1962 pg. 543 / Author; Dr. Samuel U. Rodgers)

A DECEMBER 2021 REFLECTION

Today I visited the website for the Samuel U. Rodgers Health Center as I often do, as a reminder of the outstanding work that continues today. I sat transfixed—as usual—as if it were my first website visit. Presenting via video Ms. Rosalee Watkins, prior employee, and honorable alumnus, recounts the history of the health center. She states clearly, "The thing that Dr. Rodgers was first known for in Kansas City was suing the State of Missouri."

I watch, listen, and quietly smile as usual, knowing this was just my father's opening act.

THE GOOD LIFE (1950–1965)

Practice Makes Perfect

*"It is no use walking anywhere to preach
unless our walking is our preaching."*

—FRANCES OF ASSISI

I imagine the voice of our ancestors speaking to my father:

*"One major accomplishment may not signal the end of one's quest.
Keep moving while seeking the next horizon. It was the North
Star that gave your ancestors the starting point and continuous
connections on the journey northward toward freedom. Progress
comes in small increments, with unfinished business along the way.
Keep following your North Star that will lead to your purposeful
destination. Push for reform…someone must."*

PROFESSIONAL PRACTICE AND CERTIFICATIONS; HUMANS AND HEROES, KANSAS CITY, MISSOURI

I remained amazed at the level of accomplishment, the hard-fought battles won and sometimes lost. The selfless sacrifice and family sacrifice required of these African American physicians throughout their lives. The intellectual brilliance of this group of men was lost to me as a child. I now wondered if my father documented his medical journey along the way, knowing that I and others would find these treasures when we could fully appreciate them.

When I visited the clinic as a child, I could find my way easily to each of their offices in the newly constructed building, and I knew their medical specialties. Some brought babies into the world, others removed tonsils, others took care of children. What I knew for sure is they were family. They were uniquely funny. I could reimagine their personalities from my arsenal of childhood memories. They were resourceful, respectful, and brave. Never did I know in the moment how courageous and brilliant they were. They masked their incredible credentials with such humility and kindness. Jim Crow narrowed the pipeline of their lives and options, progressively funneling down to limited choices.

Dr. Carl Peterson hailed from Alabama and sported a bald head and plaid bow tie—so popular today—like no one else. Dr. Filmore Haith had a heart so big you could see it beating a mile away, with a dry "Dom DeLuise" sense of humor that would "catch you off guard" every time. He could make you laugh without trying, and his kindness was unforgettable. Dr. Starks Williams, ever so kind, greeted children with important questions that made you feel as if you were the only one that mattered, no baby talk included. Dr. W. R. Peterson was tall, slim, and debonair—a Fred Astaire type character. I was the "Ginger Rogers" and dance partner at five years old when my parents entertained at our home. I could "cut the rug" as I danced the "Madison" and did the "twist" on one foot, knee raised in the air, to Chubby Checker.

The "Madison" was the line dance of the late 1950s, and I knew every step. My father captured these party scenes on reel-to-reel film, as Dr. Peterson—three times my height—held my hand as he slowly turned me around. A night owl, I stayed awake as long as I could, usually falling asleep in the arms of a guest and awaking the next morning in my bed. The guests received unexpected entertainment, and the reel-to-reel film footage provided family laughter for years to come.

Does the world make men like this anymore? I wondered. I am grateful they organized as brothers to defeat racism.

Most importantly SUR wrote of their historic victories and difficulties at GH2 as a blueprint for all people of color to overcome adversity. Individual physicians as contributing writers were assigned specific topics within the *JNMA*. Now as I write, I am determined they will never be forgotten.

REFLECTIONS ON AN ATLANTA, GEORGIA EVENING

On the evening of December 20, 2021, I opened my file drawer full of collected memories to find a yellow folder. It was filled with old paperwork, handwritten notes from my sister, yellowed newspaper articles, etc. I carefully slid the materials from the envelope in anticipation—the final amazement at the uncovering of materials I never remembered reading. The contents of this envelope, taken from my memory box, filled in more pieces of the puzzle. My memory supplied the rest.

I hesitated with the anticipation of a child unwrapping a Christmas gift. I had already predicted the greatness of the gift. I carefully handled each yellowed newspaper, as if it might disintegrate before my eyes. These were precious, priceless time capsules of history. I was energized to continue writing supplemented by these treasures, some written by the storytellers themselves. It was now my turn to pass the baton of history to others, my contribution the easier task by far. I was reminded of a quote.

"As writers, what we do is remember. And to remember this world is to create it."

TONY MORRISON

"As I See It" article

THE DOCTORS' CLINIC: A SLOW PROCESS, 1949

The first document uncovered from the pile was a newspaper article in the 1954 *Kansas City Star* entitled "As I See It: Integration of KC hospitals Was a Slow Process," by Dr. Starks Williams. I had no recollection of having read this article until now—one of the many documents I was copied on, filed, and never read. However, I knew the story by heart. I smiled slowly at the sight of Dr. Starks Williams' photograph before I could begin reading. I quickly refocused on the content of the article, as my mind wanted to lead me down memory lane. I saw the faces of his wife and family, his home and our visits there, and the sound of his deep lilting voice. I had special memories of all my father's colleagues. Dr. William's specialty of pediatrics was one that did not need much explanation for a kid. I knew my father ensured babies were born and Dr. Williams took care of them after they arrived.

The doctors' clinic: 25th and Brooklyn colleagues celebrate new practice

The original doctors' clinic was located at 25th Street and Brooklyn Avenue (2462-A Brooklyn Avenue), in the heart of the black community, on the second floor of a red brick building conveniently above a drugstore. I remembered being in the back seat of my parents' car where my siblings and I would entertain ourselves as we waited outside in the car. In the days of 1950s doctor's house calls, we would ride along on weekends. If we had time between patients, we might negotiate a visit to a candy store along the way and certainly on the way home. It was more than fun, I realized years later. I would see my father at work, his diligence and importance in addressing the needs of his patients, and their gratefulness for it all.

Dr. Williams came to Kansas City in 1954, to join the doctors' clinic opened five years prior. He was welcomed by the group of four, Doctors Sam Rodgers, W.R. Peterson, Carl Peterson, and John Ramos. Although new to this practice, "Starks" was already a "brother" of the team of four. "All of us were on staff at GH2 and we assimilated or integrated GH1 with GH2," said Dr. Starks Williams in a 1954 interview with the *Kansas City Star.*

In Kansas City, black doctors and black patients could only go to two places, GH2 and Wheatley-Provident Hospital at 18th Street and Forest Avenue. "I couldn't even go into GH1." Dr. Williams explained the effort of the young doctors getting board certified, a better place to practice, and a better opportunity as a "little upheaval in Kansas City." Williams acknowledged "good will on both sides" when the segregated hospitals were eventually merged over a miraculous period of one to two years. (1954 Article KC Star "Integration of KC hospitals was a slow process," Dr. Starks Williams)

I smiled again reminded of the humility, courage, and self-confidence of this group of men who had collectively changed history. I believe their ancestral faith in a higher power "bubble-wrapped" them from harm and unproductive behaviors and blessed them with protection to accomplish historically monumental feats. They banded together and took it all in stride. This fierce stamina would serve them well professionally and improve race relations in Kansas City.

JACKSON COUNTY MEDICAL SOCIETY:
A SEAT AT THE TABLE, 1950

Sometimes when you deserve a seat at the table you must create your own seat and your own table when it doesn't exist for you. History had taught this group of gallant men to persist and create non-existing opportunities. In their usual way, I imagined them thinking again "keep moving" as they had always done.

In the jointly written Journal of the National Medical Association organized by my father, a contributor wrote, "The Kansas City Medical Society (KCMS) was organized to represent the Negro Physicians of the community before the members were accepted into the various other medical societies." At its formation the KCMS was composed of forty-seven active members who were residents in training. There were many goals established but one of the most important was "to sponsor the enactment of just medical laws, and to eliminate religious and racial discrimination and segregation from American medical institutions." (Volume 34, No. 5—Kansas City General Hospital No. 2—pg. 539).

A *Kansas City Star* article, "Inter-Racial Milestone," explained the first six Negro physicians were elected to membership of the Jackson County Medical Society (JCMS) abolishing the seventy-year racial requirement to be white.

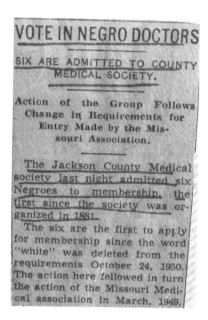

Vote in Negro Doctors—JCMS

The *Kansas City Star* October 24, 1955, article "Vote in Negro Doctors," reads, "The JCMS society last night admitted six Negroes to membership, the first since the society was organized in 1881. The six are the first to apply for membership since the word "white" was deleted from the requirements October 24, 1950." The long-standing admission rules of the society required a physician's application be published three times, at which time any member could object. The second step required the unanimous approval by the board of censors and the affirmation of the eighteen-member executive council of the society. "The executive council took such action last night at a regular monthly meeting in the society offices in the Argyle

Building." The article listed "The Negroes" admitted along with their home addresses:

1. Dr. Bruce P. McDonald
2. Dr. Carl M. Peterson
3. Dr. Walter R. Peterson
4. Dr. John F. Ramos, Jr.
5. Dr. Samuel U. Rodgers
6. Dr. Luke E. Williams

The band of brother physicians added yet another "first" to their resumes. I added a few more motivational words to my meditation vocabulary. "Be always ready! Anticipate the next step even when it is not on the table for you. Your dream can be transformed into a reality." I would close my eyes and say out loud and alone, "Dream, keep moving, be ready, anticipate."

Notably, three (C. M. Peterson, W. R. Peterson and S. U. Rodgers) of the six listed were already practicing physicians at the newly established doctors' clinic. These physicians all lived and worked in the black community. Their practices, churches, and social networks were there, providing strength and support for them, and those that witnessed their example. It was their strength of example and expectation that their existence modeled for others—the same expectation my father's parents modeled for him.

Education was expectation number one in the Rodgers clan. I paused and reminisced about the small town of Anniston where Ulysses had grown up, where big men came from small places, where he had more than his share of positive and aspirational role models.

These courageous men were "dragon slayers" in my mind. I imagined all six standing firmly atop a mountain with their faces turned upward to the sky, always prepared, seeking the next horizon. I didn't watch much *Superman* nor read the comic books so popular in the 1950s and 1960s for hero identification. I wasn't in search of additional heroes. I already knew quite a few.

AMERICAN BOARD OF OBSTETRICS AND GYNECOLOGY (ABOG), 1953

In 1953, the good news was shared in a local newspaper article entitled "Dr. Samuel U. Rodgers Passes American Board": (The Kansas City Star, 1953.)

ABOG News Article

"Dr. Samuel U. Rodgers, 36, 1322 E. 22nd St., one of the four physicians affiliated with the Doctor's Clinic, 2462 Brooklyn, was notified Tuesday that he had successfully passed the American Board of Obstetrics and Gynecology ('ABOG') examination which he completed May 15."

The article further detailed, "Dr. Rodgers was the first negro of Kansas City to be certified specifically by the ABOG." The article reported "all three of the ABOG members are affiliated with the Doctor's Clinic." In 1950, Dr. John F. Ramos (radiology) and Dr. Carl M. Peterson (surgery) also passed.

In the 1998 Atlanta interview in his early '80s, my father described Kansas City (GH1 and GH2) as a unique situation with unique medical opportunities. He explained, "As a result, I became the first black doctor to become a medical examiner for the ABOG."

Lastly the interviewer asked, "What has brought you the greatest pleasure?"

"Professionally?" he clarified. Then without hesitation, he went on, "The opportunities I had to be trained by the best OB-GYN physicians in the country; there was no excuse for failure after these opportunities." He still recognized the significance of this Kansas City migration move years later.

JUST KEEP MOVING
Simply reading SUR's accomplishments achieved over sixteen years was both mind boggling and thought provoking. I thought about the barrier-breaking effort it had taken for

each accomplishment. I imagined swimming frantically to the water's surface for air, all while being chained to a sunken boat at the bottom of the ocean. There were no turnkey accomplishments in my father's life. It involved venturing into the unknown, the dismantling of racial barriers every step of the way, migration, relocation, disappointment, and delay at every turn. How did he do it?

"The fall of dropping water wears away the stone."
LUCRETIUS

I believe the key to my father's success was that he just kept moving. My father kept believing, perceiving, seeking, dreaming, and knowing that water finds the path of least resistance. It seemed that everything he put his hand to eventually turned to gold, through his continued defiance of society's norms. There was no stagnation in his determination or hesitation in his mind, body, or spirit. He simply kept moving through the storms. I closed my eyes and whispered twice, "If we just keep moving forward, we will meet our dreams head on." My father fulfilled his dream to become a trained surgeon. What more was there to want, and what more would it take?

FAMILY EXPECTATIONS

In the Rodgers clan there were no exceptions to knowing and understanding family expectations from the youngest to the oldest. Some expectations were spoken; many were not. You were never home free from at least trying to achieve. In 1944, upon Gordon, Jr.'s. return to Anniston following WWII, he announced to his parents he would take a respite before officially starting his dental practice. His mother, Fannie Mamie, had arranged the purchase of the house next door at 1616 Cooper Avenue.

"It's a perfect location for your practice; and it will be available for you to start as soon as possible," I can imagine my grandmother saying.

Often when we are ready to stop, others ensure we keep moving. When Fannie Mamie said it, it was in the making or already done. The rule of expectation applied to one and all.

My self-content sister Rita at age five never bothered a soul and found comfort in sucking her thumb while reading. Rita was the spitting image of my father in demeanor, looks, disposition, and intellect. She was quiet with big expressive eyes that spoke volumes. During our annual summer Anniston visit of 1961, my grandmother warned her of the "future tooth perils" that thumb sucking brings. My grandmother applied a harmless bitter tasting ointment to her thumb to discourage this practice. Undaunted, my sister looked on, then switched to the opposite thumb by summer's end. In the summer of 1962, my grandmother visited us in Kansas City.

When my father happily announced, "Your grandmother's coming for a visit this summer," my sister looked on wide-eyed, absorbing the news. Miraculously without prompting, the thumb sucking ceased before my grandmother arrived, never to be seen again.

Often when we are ready to stop, others ensure we keep moving in the direction of truth. Expectation is a mighty motivator coming from someone who loves you. Decades later in her forties, my sister would express her gratitude for knowing the expectation always set before us. In breaking down racial barriers, my father ruffled many feathers, but succeeded with total and resolute inner peace. Change is difficult, but in the end the known truth about life will set you—and others—free to keep moving.

The Miracle

QUEEN OF THE WORLD

Sometimes it takes a miracle, and the story of the work carried out at "Queen of the World Hospital" (QOTW) was nothing less. The historic progress achieved at QOTW represented a major breakthrough in specialty training for black physicians. QOTW had played a major role in my father's life story, and the QOTW thread would continue in mine.

In 1983, I moved to New York for a corporate opportunity and settled initially in Hastings on Hudson, Westchester County. My last county move was further north to Ossining, New York, a beautiful and secluded place known to most outsiders as the home of the Sing Sing Correctional Facility. I made my home at Eagle Bay. Ossining was an idyllic, mountainous retreat far enough away from the hustle and bustle of New York City, where you might see deer in your yard anytime of the day.

My mother passed away during my few years in NY, and following her death, my father visited NY several times. It was a lonely and disorienting time for us all, but we had each other. I would wake every morning thinking to call her, to be abruptly reminded that my mother, my anchor, was gone. As my father and I walked through the theater district of NY amid the grime and filth, my father turned to me and asked, "Why would anyone want to live here?" I was young and adaptable enough to find it all a joyous adventure in my mid-twenties, despite the lingering odors of rotted trash that followed us as we strolled.

"It's certainly a different world from what I'm accustomed to," I replied, trying to convince myself.

As usual, my father knew someone from his college days everywhere we traveled. New York was no exception, and we ended the day dining at a Talladega College schoolmate's brownstone home in Harlem. It was a delightful evening of story-swapping between old college friends. My father shared stories about his New York days in his early twenties, working summers as a busboy on the big steamers and cruise ships docked in the harbor. I now felt welcome and at home in New York.

To familiarize myself with my new Ossining neighborhood, I took a walk down the secluded two-lane road. Shortly, I arrived at a wide driveway—literally next door—that appeared to lead to nowhere. I saw no buildings or signage in clear sight. Curious, I decided to follow the winding drive, until I entered what appeared to be a wildlife preserve that offered a peace and calm, I couldn't describe. I stood still and took a panoramic view of my surroundings—all trees and flowers—suddenly seeing a sign that read "Maryknoll Sisters" and I wondered no more. I knew for sure that the

Maryknoll Sisters were "family"—my family. I felt at once safe and at home. I felt I had landed in heaven. In a 1955 newspaper article I found in 2021, this area was referred to as "Maryknoll N.Y., 55 Ryder Road-Ossining N.Y., located 35 miles from New York City." (The Kansas City Times, "No Medical Bar," May 23, 1955.) The serendipity of life was alive and well. Twenty years later I was living next door to the miracle-making Maryknoll Sisters in Ossining, sisters I had come to know very well during my childhood.

THE MARYKNOLL MISSION

Curious, I Googled their website. Per the "Maryknoll - An International Catholic Mission Movement" website, "Maryknoll, a Catholic non-profit mission movement has been the heart and hands of the US Catholic Church's overseas mission work for more than 100 years. Maryknoll Sisters give witness to God's love and devote our lives in service overseas helping the poor, the ailing and the marginalized." The Maryknoll Sisters began their mission in 1912, becoming the first group of US Catholic sisters founded for overseas mission. (The Kansas City Times, 1955.)

From as early as I can remember, I considered them angels. In 1955—the year of my birth—the Maryknoll Sisters arrived in the inner city of Kansas City to "help the poor, the ailing and the marginalized." I am convinced that God's love brought them there. Their website slogan read, "Maryknoll Sisters—Making God's Love Visible," and indeed, they did.

Integration is a slow process. Even after the major hospital desegregation milestone was achieved, there was still much more to do in creating health care equality for black doctors, staff, and patients. Change requires that good people get and stay involved until the mission is accomplished.

Catholic Archbishop Edwin O'Hara invited the Maryknoll overseas mission to come to Kansas City, where he had tried to integrate catholic hospitals St. Joseph's and St. Mary's hospitals to little avail. As Dr. Williams explained, "They set up two beds in each hospital for black physicians. If you had three patients one of them couldn't go into that hospital."

What do you do when you've done all you can? My mind drifted back to the lyrics of the song "Stand" by artist Donnie McClurkin.

THE MAGIC KINGDOM

By the age of four, I couldn't remember life without the Queen of the World Hospital. This hospital was a big part of my world and that of many others. It was where my father delivered babies, saw patients, and perfected his specialty in OB-GYN. It was a magical place with a befitting name. "Queen of the World," I would proclaim with a giggle. Fortunately, the name contained no R's, which caused me grave difficulty in pronouncing. The name rolled easily off my tongue and was equally fun to say. It was much easier to pronounce than my brother and sister's names, which both began with the letter R. The magical name alone fit nicely in my universe of princesses and queens, as I was learning and mesmerized by the popular Walt Disney fairytales.

As a family we spent a good deal of time in or around QOTW: my father as staff, my mother as a women's auxiliary member and volunteer, my brother Rickey (age ten) and I (age seven) as tonsillectomy patients and hospital roommates in 1962.

One afternoon while on patient rounds my father stopped by. The look on his face was priceless. I imagined the proverbial bubble floating overhead that read, "Whose kids are these... They can't be mine!"

He was startled by the numerous mounds of tissues littered throughout the room and the overflowing trash cans. "We tried to clean up," I told him.

I paused and looked up for a moment, then continued my coloring. I had determined to finish coloring Wilma Flintstone's red hair before the nurses brought my afternoon Jell-O. My brother whined to go home; my father looked on with his normal cool. We all secretly wished my mother was there to make it all better, as she always did. This hospital experience was a lesson in appreciation for Elizabeth Rodgers, who dealt every day in the realm of unpredictability with three young children, an OB-GYN husband whose schedule was predicated on mother nature, no nurses, doctors, nor kitchen/custodial staff. My mother was a Wonder Woman. My father knew this and loved her for this reason and so many more.

I was born in March of 1955 and my sister in August of 1956 at QOTW, delivered by my father's mentor Dr. Harold Gainey. My father held Dr. Gainey in highest esteem for many reasons. Dr. Gainey became an essential part of the solution versus the problem; at a time in this country's racial history when many white physicians had not or would not. Dr. Gainey had a track record of experience having been at General Hospital No. 2 before and during the desegregation effort.

It would take decades for me to appreciate and know the full history, which was the real magic of QOTW. It was not a fairytale, but nothing short of a miracle. I share the miraculous story today and will continue for the rest of my life. I owe this to the many who sacrificed, who listened and followed the divine, who believed all people deserve equitable health care, who held steadfast to a dream not waiting on the how but believing it would somehow manifest. I wished I could thank them all in person for their gallant efforts, but that time is gone. I desire for the writing of this story to become my first installment of continued gratitude. It is my forever example of divine intervention and what is possible when all hearts beat on one accord.

I shudder thinking about my father's uncontained joy having experienced the miracles of QOTW. He experienced the birth of his children and attained his ultimate dream of specialty training to become a surgeon. He met a mentor in Dr. Harry Gainey, forming a lifelong friendship that led to his certification in the ABOG. Gainey was honored posthumously in the SURHC Fiftieth Anniversary Program honorees listing, as having been "instrumental to Dr. Rodgers becoming a licensed OB-GYN." My mind briefly visited the make believe—what if—warehouse of near-missed dreams. I honored the serendipity of my father's life journey, accepting that life's every detail can never be planned.

I will tell others of how a missionary order of nuns landed in Kansas City, as if it were a third-world country to "help the poor, the ailing, and the marginalized." The sisters—nurses and doctors—were my earliest example of women in charge in the workplace. They were kind, competent, firm, determined and took charge. These sisters were as determined and experienced on the front lines of adversity as were my father and his colleagues. They teamed together and became a force to be reckoned with. What were the odds that a worldwide missionary order would arrive in Kansas City to do the impossible? I believe God orders our steps and intervenes in ways we have yet to understand. It is my father's lived testimony of what is made possible when all hearts beat on one accord. Miraculous progress is only made possible with a change in the hearts of those who agree to a greater goal.

SISTER MADELINE MARIA

In 1952, Sister Madeline Maria, RN and administrator, would write about a community group who suggested to Archbishop O'Hara that a hospital be provided for Negroes. "I am not interested in a Negro Hospital. I will suggest that the hospital open its doors to all persons regardless of race, color, or creed," O'Hara said. Even so, as Sister Madeline Maria reported it took three years to convince the General Hospital that integration was possible and desirable at QOTW.

"After much debate and long delays GH finally closed the segregated hospital unit and one after the other of its services integrated. During the last years of delay by GH, private hospitals in Kansas City made at least a token effort to increase integration," she wrote. Menorah Hospital was noted as "outstanding" in its early efforts to integrate, with six Negro doctors on staff and a 5 percent Negro patient admitting rate. (Citing New: JNMA, 1962.)

QOTW played a critical bridging role in the interim period following the closing of segregated hospitals GH1 and GH2, when no hospitals existed that would accommodate an integrated physician staff and patient population. QOTW created a safe space solution, until the eventual integration of hospitals throughout Kansas City, enabling SUR and his medical colleagues to continue their specialty training non-stop.

The courage of these "sisters and brother physicians" was historically significant; the impact of their faithful accomplishments produced rippling effects of racial progress. Shortly after the Bishop's proclamation of service for all, the thirty-two-bed St. Vincent's Maternity Hospital (SVMH), the facility that pre-dated QOTW on the same site, was replaced by the renovated one-hundred-bed general hospital, which was named QOTW. Most importantly this effort had also given the city a hospital where white doctors could take their Negro patients and Negro doctors could take their white patients. This hospital was the only interracial, non-sectarian hospital in Kansas City at the time. "With the progress made so far, it is hoped that the two hospitals (GH1, GH2) still segregated will soon open their doors and that the others, whose doors are now just ajar, will throw them wide open," said Sister Madeline Maria. It was an avalanche of blessings enough to break the dam of indifference after a decade of effort.

DR. STARKS WILLIAMS

Archbishop O'Hara established a group to assess the limited bed situation. "There was a thirty-two-bed foundling hospital at 23rd Street and College Avenue (SVMH) for unwed mothers." "They rebuilt it with Hill-Burton money and funds raised in the community and called it Queen of the World."

In 1965, Dr. Starks Williams would recall that because of the steadfastness of many, in time, all staff of QOTW had privileges not only at St. Joseph's and St. Mary's hospitals, but additionally at Trinity Lutheran Hospital. The two-bed restriction was lifted with the integration of Christian hospitals. In the meantime, the first hospital in the larger community that opened its doors to black patients was miraculously "Menorah," a Jewish hospital, the ram in the bush. Additionally, Menorah invited black physicians, nurses, technicians, and staff to join their staffs.

Queen of the World closed in 1965, ten years after it opened, making record progress in health care and human rights. It opened officially on May 22, 1955. Among the active medical staff of thirty-four physicians, twenty-five were Negroes; 8 dentists, 7 of whom are Negroes and Courtesy Staff of 175, 8 of whom are Negroes, giving a total of forty-one Negro doctors on a total staff of 258, the sister documented. "We think that the example of professional men working together in harmony has been an inspiration to a large number of doctors. The white doctors who originally formed the nucleus of QOTW remain as interested today in the welfare and success of the Negro physicians and hospital, and continue to give loyal support," wrote Sister Madeline Maria. (Journal of the National Medical Association, 1962.)

QOTW is the proof that miracles do happen when good people prevail. It takes a village of people with humane determination.

Queen of the World Hospital

CITY COUNCIL RESOLUTION CLOSES GH2, 1957

My father wrote, "In November of 1957, the City Council Resolution No. 22046 voted as a measure of economy to consolidate all the city hospitals, with no social pressure from outside." This resolution spelled the official end to GH2, resulting in the total integration of all patients, professional and non-professional personnel. As space would allow at GH1, all Negro patients, medical staff, and non-professional staff were transferred to the once all-white GH1. The last clinical service that remained at GH2 was obstetrics and gynecology, which was eventually transferred upon completion of the new facility in early 1963. (Journal of the National Medical Association, 1962.)

Dr. Williams described the 1957 city ordinance that put the two hospitals together: "No. 1 was up on Hospital Hill...No. 2 was down in the valley both very rigidly segregated." It was a befitting analogy knowing in the minds of my father and colleagues, these were matters worth elevating and fighting for as they already had. Old habits and attitudes that separate people die a centuries-long death. It wasn't over yet. Sometimes it takes a miracle.

Simply the Best

THE NEW DOCTOR'S CLINIC

On February 4, 1961, the *Kansas City Star* headlines read, "WILL OPEN NEW CLINIC—DOCTORS GROUP PLANS EVENT NEXT SUNDAY—Six Physicians Are in Medic Facility at 31st and Montgall Street."

The official newspaper announcement came late, as the "community grapevine" was already in effect. These hero physicians were renowned and embraced by their community. If you were an African American Kansas Citian in the 1960s receiving medical treatment, chances are it was through the expert care of the "dynamic six." They were beloved sons of the community. I continue to hear stories of the multi-generational babies delivered by Dr. Sam Rodgers and Dr. Filmore Haith. The rare exception was if they had not.

"Your father delivered my children and grandchildren," they would say beaming with pride, confirming a memorable experience.

The doctors' clinic, 31st & Montgall St.

The doctors' clinic (reception)

In 1960, the group of African American men who aspired to be the "best doctors" moved into a newly constructed doctors' clinic. In the *JNMA* article "Group Practice in Kansas City," Drs. W. R. Peterson and W. F. Haith wrote, "All are certified by a specialty board, or are board certified. Para-medical personnel and business office staff total 10, among whom are two registered pharmacists. Associated with us are a part-time radiologist, certified public accountant, and legal counsel. In December 1960, we moved to our present modern facilities. We are in the 13th year of operation, and at this time see no overt sign of misfortune or cause to abandon this growing facet of medicine, group practice." (JNMA_Vol, 54, No.5-Kansas City General Hospital No. 2-Group Practice in Kansas City, pg. 543.)

The *Journal of the National Medical Association* was a detailed historical summary written by Samuel U. Rodgers, MD, in September of 1962 documenting the history of Kansas City General Hospital No. 1 for whites, and General Hospital No. 2 for Negroes. Dr. Rodgers supplemented his story with integration developments in other hospitals/medical areas in Kansas City. In this effort Rodgers invited the assistance of four contributing authors.

Queen of the World Hospital: Sister Madeline Marie

Kansas City Medical Society: Dr. James S. Jackson

Group Practice in Kansas City: Drs. W.R. Peterson and W.F. Haith

The Doctors Clinic, Kansas City, Missouri

Doctors' clinic, *JNMA*

The doctors' clinic was described in the *JNMA* article as "the cutting edge" of integration and modern medicine in our community. It was the first time we had a group of minorities, all highly qualified. (Vol, 54, No.5-Kansas City General Hospital No. 2,-pg. 543.)

The *KC Star* news article emphasized a different aspect: "Six Negro physicians own and operate the clinic, described as the first of its kind established and operated as a partnership. The Doctor's clinic formerly occupying second floor quarters at 2462 Brooklyn Avenue, will formally open its new and modern building."

In 1960, the formal opening of the doctors' clinic was the talk of the town. Although just six years old, I remember the excitement of that day. Congratulatory flowers were delivered and strategically placed throughout the clinic and our home. Photographers showed up in both places, and my Anniston grandmother arrived for the special occasion. Showcased on my father's desk was a new picture of his children, known as the Three R's (Rickey, Rosalyn, and Rita) in our latest dance recital attire. Years later, patients would ask, "Dr. Rodgers are these your grandchildren?" He'd knowingly chuckle and attempt to clarify the confusion, although the picture remained.

This new clinic was truly an architectural gem. The 5,800-square-foot, air-conditioned structure housed private offices, a diagnostic and treatment center, exam and x-ray rooms, labs, lounge, and a small pharmacy. The *Kansas City Star* stated, "John Lawrence Daw of Roark, Daw & See, architects designed the contemporary structure, employing considerable colors inside and out." (Kansas City Star, Sunday, February 5, 1961) I would remember most the special blue glass and white-and-orange accent panels described in the article. Two decades later, I would do my architectural internship with John Daw.

"We weren't aspiring to be the best black doctors in town; we were aspiring to be the best doctors."

DR. STARKS WILLIAMS

My parents celebrated unheard-of victories throughout their lives. I marveled at the balance they managed to establish in our family life. They were a team respected by entire communities for their down-to-earth qualities. They experienced first-time professional achievements as a black couple—with both feet planted on solid ground. Most everyone wanted to know them, and many confided in them. Though members of many social organizations, they were unassuming homebodies at heart and took many people's secrets to their graves. They were beloved and trusted.

Like most children, our home life revolved around the Three R's. We had no idea that the Daddy we saw return home every day had just transformed a little more of the world and community through his compassion and love he showered daily on his family.

FAMILY LIFE AT 3405 QUINCY

My parents loved children. Well, you may say, "Who doesn't?" Indeed, most parents love their "own" children, but my parents loved theirs and everyone else's. I say this with conviction, as in the first decade of their marriage they were unable to conceive. However, the desire to parent never left their hearts.

Professionally, my father was heralded throughout Kansas City, forever on a pedestal in the eyes of his patients, many who thought motherhood would never happen for them. The pouring of accolades would nearly dominate the evening at any formal affair attended by my parents.

"Oh... Dr. Rodgers I want to thank you again."

"I will never forget; becoming a mother was a dream come true."

These women would share stories of the blessings of parenthood and their bundle of joy, made possible through the specialized training of Dr. Rodgers after they had tried everything they could, along with the grace of God. My parents, after ten years of hoping and waiting, loved children so much they decided to adopt. They were in good company as several of my father's medical colleagues and friends did the same.

Baby Richard

Life continued, and they adopted my brother Richard, born April 2, 1952. I learned his full birth name of "Richard Johnson" when I was clearing out my father's safety deposit box after his passing. I don't believe my brother ever asked. They called him "Rickey," and he came with a head full of curly hair, big eyes, and bowed legs, which they dealt with through corrective surgery. Rickey's first birthday celebrated with my parents was age two. I remember the old film footage of him on the floor, before crawling through the center of the cake. I remember too, the heavy steel casts with the wraparound leather banding he wore until his legs were healed. He later became an avid swimmer and beautiful diver, all aided by the intervention of early surgery. My parents were so elated about their new parental status that they proceeded to arrange the second adoption to our family, a little girl.

Life is unpredictable. As my parents contemplated another adoption, they learned they were expecting. I imagined the excitement of my father's OB-GYN partner, Filmore Haith, who more than likely broke the good news-immediately in real time. I imagined Dr. Haith finally saying, "Sam, I've got great news!" after first cloaking the message in his characteristic off-beat humor.

Home of Dr. Filmore Haith

I was born March 6, 1955. My mother shared her story repeatedly: "Early on I told no one—not even my mother. I just couldn't believe it myself, after all these years!" Some say good fortune comes in spades, and on August 5, 1956, my baby sister Rita was born. We were born to a mother with one ovary and the faith of a mustard seed. Our family was now complete, and we became known as the Three R's.

Rickey was the curious and courageous one. I was the artistically creative, energetic one, and Rita the compassionate, caring bookworm. As I look in the rearview mirror of life, our interests were clear from the beginning. Our individual callings were evident from the start. My parents observed our natural inclinations and nurtured each accordingly. We benefited from each other's proclivities, and with three children within a four-year span of each other, it was easier to manage. The Three R's all took swimming, music, and dance lessons, and of course, reading and education was essential whether you liked it or not.

Rickey would roam the neighborhood, always the first to arrive at the scene of the crime, usually a fender-bender on the well-traveled Van Brunt Boulevard across from our home. Rita was always tucked away quietly reading, while the other two tore through the house.

Exposure to the arts was valued, and by age four, I was enrolled in art classes at the renowned Nelson Atkins Museum of Art. The Three R's would participate in multi-racial children's events. One of our favorites was the children's "Coke Concert," a Sunday afternoon activity held at the KC Art Institute in partnership with the Kansas City Philharmonic. I was in my element, laying in my dress on the floor, drawing for hours with a string quartet playing in the background, as I nibbled on the cookies.

Participation in the arts (music, dance, art), which made me happiest at four, remains core to my being. I gravitate toward creative processes involving seemingly unrelated elements to reimagine them, whether it be lines on paper, cooking ingredients, or people. Like my parents, I zero in on core issues with little patience for nonsense. I experience righteous indignation over the intentional maltreatment of people. My cursive S is reminiscent of my father's. I am my mother's spitting image. Like Dorothy's red shoe revelation in *The Wizard of Oz*, I've had what I needed all along. "She's never met a stranger or a recipe she couldn't change," laughs Rita. I am forever grateful for parents who let us be ourselves, providing the support to groom our natural interests.

This musical activity was in keeping with experiences at home. SUR was not a rough-and-tumble, chase-you-through-the-house father. Instead, we spent quiet afternoons on the living room floor reading before a crackling fire, as my mother prepared a grand Sunday dinner. We would listen to the fabled "Peter and the Wolf," with the distinctive tympani and oboe sounds, as my father isolated the sound of each instrument. These downtime afternoons were enjoyed by all. My mother, who loved cooking—without the Three R's underfoot—and my father, who enjoyed a reprieve from his world-saving activities.

The Christmas scene at our house reflected our personal traits and family life. Rickey the protector received a cap gun/holster, Rita a doctor's bag, and I an artist painting set. I can still easily conjure up the magical Christmas scenes in our home decades later. I would realize as I grew older that it was not the bedazzling Christmas tree with the colorful blinking lights that made it magical. It was the love that always permeated our home—the "love light" that neighbors, cousins, friends, and strangers were forever drawn to like a moth to the light.

IN DUE TIME

One early 4 a.m. Christmas morning, the Three R's tip-toed down the steps in the dark to our living room. The aromas of fresh pine, homemade Christmas cookies, and fireplace timber lingered in the air. Rickey, the tallest, would perform the honor of flipping on the light switch to reveal a magical space of sparkly lights, a stocking hung fireplace, candy-cane-draped Christmas tree, and a room full of toys. Dressed alike as usual, Rita and I wore candy cane flannel pajamas and black eyes from a swing set accident, entered the room. On this Christmas day, Rita's fourth, she received several memorable gifts. She sported her cowboy boots, hat, and holster/play gun that rested on her hip, influenced by the Roy Rogers & Dale Evans cowboy show watched with my brother. Then with our relatives gathered for Christmas brunch, I believe Rita discovered her calling.

Resting under the tree was another small package that contained a toy doctors' bag. It was bright orange and held a plastic stethoscope with green tubing and a bottle of colorful candy pills. Having watched my father, she recognized the stethoscope and knew exactly what to do. With it draped around her neck in a room of family members, she began walking from one relative to the other. Silently asking, with expressive eyes only, she compassionately placed the stethoscope near their hearts and patiently paused, turning her head slightly to listen for a heartbeat. The adults looked on with amused curiosity, but there was no laughter. They recognized the significance of this moment, as even I did. Rita was a southpaw and so much like my father in every way. "She's a Rodgers," they would say. The rest would become history in due time.

Rita acknowledged decades later, "There were early unspoken expectations that set my career path in place, early in life. We were exposed to cultural events while also being grounded in the realities of our community.

The Good Fight

CIVIL RIGHTS

By the age of seven, I was fully exposed to the civil rights effort. My vocabulary included names like George Wallace, Bull Connor, and stories about MLK, Snow White, Bambi, and Emmett Till. I knew who was good and bad in the fairytales and in real life. In Miss Virginia's own words from the 1950s *Romper Room* television show—the 1950s *Sesame Street*—there were "Do-Bees and Don't-Bees," and I learned the difference. I also learned later that we all had a choice about who we wanted to be – good or evil.

I first learned about racism and hatred and how to combat it in the front parlor of my Anniston grandparents' loving home. The political activism of the Rodgers family exposed them as ready targets for southern white supremacists. In this room I would watch the evening news with my granddaddy. I would watch George Wallace's actions at the University of Alabama, the 16th Street Baptist Church bombing (1963, Montgomery, Alabama) that killed four little girls who looked like me. The *JET* magazine featuring the cover story of Emmett Till sat on the coffee table. The Mississippi lynching and kidnapping of Emmitt Till occurred in August of 1955, five months after my birth. Till's story of torture was kept alive in the black community, and by the age of seven I could read every word of the *JET* magazine article. The image of his battered face on the front cover still haunts me today.

These victims were all murdered in their childhood while attending church or visiting their relatives in the South, just as I did every summer. I never asked my parents, "Why?" I read their facial expressions and instinctively knew there was no way to explain the senselessness of evil, then or now. Even so, they never taught us to hate, but instead taught ways to combat it by example.

We marched in the hot summers through the streets of Anniston for civil rights, attended the mass meetings at 17th street Baptist Church, three houses away from my grandparents. A racial reckoning was needed in Anniston, a hotbed for the civil rights movement in the '50s and '60s. On May 1, 1964, Dr. Martin Luther King, Jr., soon to receive the Nobel Peace Prize, spoke at the17th Street Baptist Church commending the work of the black leadership in Anniston specifically Minister Nimrod Reynolds of 17th Street Baptist. The distant stories of church bombings, lynchings, and threats seemed far enough away, until one day it hit home. I heard the concerned adult voices throughout the house, the whispered names, the re-enactment of the threatening phone calls. "If that coon shows up at the political rally tonight, we'll send his body back in a box," the voice said on the other end of the phone. It was the insulting call from the KKK intending to warn my Uncle Gordon. My grandmother, Fannie Mamie, fielded most of the calls received at 1618 Cooper.

MLK and group

Martin Luther King Jr., Dr. Gordon Rodgers, Jr.
(NAACP President)

My grandmother stood her ground stoically, a model of strength, courage, and dignity during these times. For years, the KKK continued to call and threaten my Anniston family. The calls ranged from veiled threats of planted bombs under the house to cross burnings that eventually manifested in my grandparents' front yard—steps away from the front porch where we posed for traditional summer family photographs. Following these threats, I heard adult whispers of a family name of "Adams." As my father was fighting to desegregate hospitals and improve health care delivery in Kansas City, his Anniston family was defending their lives on a much more primitive racial playing field. I held a lot of information in my head and mostly heart. The years and the details faded away, but with time will come closure, I hoped.

THE UPHILL, UPENDING, UNHEARD-OF BATTLE

For black families there is no time limitation to the civil rights movement, which continues and cannot yet be moved on from. Human rights have not become a second-nature entity like breathing. It is a daily and uphill force to be reckoned with when you wake and walk in black skin. This heavy weight of responsibility came knocking on the Rodgers' front door in full force in the 1950s and 1960s. There was much work to be done anywhere and everywhere in the US.

Much has been written about the heroic civil rights efforts of Gordon A. Rodgers. Jr. of the Memorable Sibling Duo. While Dr. Sam Rodgers was kicking down the doors of health care discrimination in Kansas City, the Rodgers clan in Anniston were similarly engaged on the civil rights front.

Gordon, the optimistic, fun-loving brother bravely led the way in Anniston's civil rights movement.

There was no doubt about it or choice in the matter. The entire Rodgers family was fully vested in the civil rights movement, which influenced their life choices regardless of what city they called home. Racism blanketed this country like a wildfire in dry forest land. It killed dreams of hope for many, like a boa constrictor kills its prey. Your choice was to fight it or to succumb to a shadow of a life.

In 1944, following the completion of his residency at General Hospital No. 2, Gordon returned to Anniston to begin his dental practice at 1616 Cooper Avenue, next door to his parents-the home where he and Ulysses had grown up. Making a living was challenging, even for an educated person. The Jim Crow South system did not promote Black success. "It was a matter of survival...I had enough patients to live off of." His obituary posted in the Anniston Star read "After experiencing the ideals of freedom, liberty and equality in Europe (during WW II duty), he worked tirelessly to achieve these same ideals as an American," as did his brother Sam Rodgers.

In the 1998 interview, Gordon, Jr. proudly explained, "In 1957, I became the state president of the Alabama NAACP. With my devil-may-care attitude, I took it on!" Gordon, Jr. held this office when Rosa Parks was secretary (1943) of the NAACP, during the 1955 Bus Boycott. In 1956, the state of Alabama obtained a court order banning the NAACP from doing business in the state.

In 1956, the state of Alabama obtained a court order, via the efforts of the Alabama attorney general, banning the NAACP from conducting business in the state. The NAACP agreed to comply with the injunction but defiantly contended that "these allegations appear to be efforts to deny the right of protest against intolerable and degrading treatment of citizens and to deny also the right of...legal action in the courts."

The state NAACP president, Dr. Gordon A. Rodgers, Jr., commented that the attorney general "cannot quench the quest for full citizenship by 900,000 Alabama Negroes through injunctions."

Rosa Parks Museum, Dr. Gordon A. Rodgers, Jr.

Uncle Gordon's quote and efforts are memorialized at the Rosa Parks Museum in a display. He was a lifetime member of the NAACP. As recorded in his 2007 obituary, "Doc was directly involved in voter registration efforts throughout the state from the 1950s through the 1980s. Threats and intimidation were commonplace."

RACIAL PROGRESS

Racial progress was being made in Anniston, and like the Kansas City hospital desegregation effort, progress could not come fast enough for the African American community. Phil Noble wrote, "On March 20, 1965, Dr. Gordon Rodgers and Nimrod Reynolds filed a lawsuit against Anniston Memorial Hospital seeking to end the operation of racially segregated wards." This action along with other developments was met with a "new round of white supremacists' rallies, vitriolic speeches, Klan rallies, and killings." On July 15, 1965, a rally was held at the courthouse attended by about a hundred Klansmen and sympathizers who attended to hear well-known white supremacist speakers. (*Beyond the Burning Bus*, pg. 131)

Anniston Memorial Hospital continued to loom large in the life of the Rodgers family, the hospital system that had denied SUR specialty training and access in 1944 when he returned to Anniston to practice.

It was amid this backdrop of racial horror that my grandparents would be tested once again. One evening my grandmother would field another anonymous caller who informed her that a KKK posse was heading to 1618 Cooper Avenue. I was told my grandmother responded, "I bet I can shoot straighter than you can." My prim and proper, pill-box-hat-wearing grandmother and stately grandfather retrieved their guns from the safe room. "I'll be ready when you get here," she had confidently said. In that moment they both quietly took seats in their front porch rocking chairs, guns resting across their laps, and waited.

I will be forever grateful to Phil Noble for leading the effort of the bi-racial committee, and more importantly documenting his journey through *Beyond the Burning Bus—The Civil Rights Revolution in a Southern Town*, adding another piece to my family puzzle.

My distant six-year-old memories would be confirmed decades later, ten times over. My memories of the Adams family involvement in the history of racial terror in Anniston was confirmed repeatedly as referenced not only in the book *Beyond the Burning Bus,* but through other means. Sixty years after the bus burning, I relaxed at home watching a *PBS American Experience* documentary entitled *A Film by Stanley Nelson—Freedom Riders.* I sat alone poised on the edge of my sofa in anticipation of what I knew would be another outstanding educational documentary by Stanley, a cousin of a cousin. I was prepared to be educated, but not prepared at all for the coming revelation.

As the documentary so carefully detailed the events of the Mother's Day bus burning, it ended by clearly including the participation of the Adams family. Adams, was the whispered name of my childhood memories. I learned that day never to discount any memory as they prove of personal value someday. In 2018, years after receiving the cherished writings of Phil Noble, the book still held a position of prominence on my coffee table. In the peace and quiet of the evening I picked up the book, and it opened to a page I'd never seen before. Before me were two photographs (front and side view) of a man. Stunned, I stared wide-eyed in total disbelief. The caption read, "Police photos of Kenneth Adams, about 1963." Phil Noble wrote, "Local KKK leader Kenneth Adams's name was synonymous with much of the racial violence in the Anniston area and even in Birmingham." (BBB pg. 126) What I thought were my childhood imaginings were reality after all.

I later met Phil Noble on possibly one of the most unforgettable days of his life, and thanked him profusely for his dedicated work toward the betterment of race relations in Anniston. It was August 10, 2012, the day of his wife Betty Noble's funeral service at Decatur Presbyterian Church. In 2021, as I began this writing, I discovered the church program tucked away with other keepsakes in my memory box. I read again the program scripture that spoke to me that day and thought of my family.

Make every effort to add to your faith, virtue; and to virtue, knowledge; and to knowledge, self-control; and to self-control, perseverance; and to perseverance, godliness; and to godliness, mutual affection; and to mutual affection, love.

II PETER 1:5–7

As the years went by, the life-threatening phone calls to my grandmother subsided in intensity and quantity. The voice on the other end of the phone instead began to speak of and share personal tragedies with my grandmother seeking mercy and benefiting from her grace and forgiveness.

The truth has a way of finding you if you just give it time. Leadership with integrity depends on truth as its core. Have patience in knowing the truth is worth the wait.

THE VISION
(1965–1993)

The Calling

"Love your calling with passion. It is the meaning of your life."

AUGUSTE RODIN

Does achieving major accomplishments deliver you to the "Promised Land"?

The underground railroad, a network of continuous connections on the journey northward, extended through Northern states to the promised land of Canada. People known as conductors guided the enslaved. It was the North Star that gave them the starting point and continuous connections on the journey northward. SUR had become a conductor achieving many "firsts" and guiding others along the way in the civil rights world of health care.

THE PROMISED LAND

An anomaly is defined as "something that deviates from what is standard, normal, or expected." (Oxford Dictionary) This was an apt description of my father's life to date. It was doubly applicable when my father decided to return to student life and then returned to Kansas City to start a new life and to establish a health center. This unusual move was indeed an anomaly in the medical world where most physicians owning lucrative practices would have remained there. SUR became an anomaly at the University of Michigan as well, as a fifty-year-old student. As my father continued to achieve great strides in the world of medicine, home life continued. Our family life would change with a few serendipitous interludes. How do you walk away from the "good life" and into the unknown?

Echoes of the Atlanta interview came slowly to my memory. I returned in my mind to the quiet of the Mayfair Library in the fall of 1998. "We all worked at my father's pharmacy over time. Uncle Gordon was the top soda jerk. In the winter part of the job was to re-bottle cough syrup brought in five-gallon containers; we had to put it in bottles, label it, and sell it for twenty-five cents. Nobody could pay you; that's why I went into public health," my father explained. Gordon chimed in with his usual and characteristic humor, "He sent a daughter to medical school so she could come back and help him."

Early memories are often haunting and keep a tight grip on our lives, until we wrestle them aside by fulfilling that ultimate calling. Perhaps God gifts us with these reckonings early in life so we have a lifetime to achieve our ultimate call.

"Samuel, a.k.a. 'Butch', and brother Gordon Jr., possessed a sprinkling of what their father had," Cousin Horace explained at the 2017 Rodgers reunion. "He was a doctor who had a drugstore with an office behind his pharmacy. He was always willing to reach down to help others, and Butch had that same quality."

After WWII, President Lyndon Johnson and the Great Society movement desired to provide accessible health care nationwide. Ten regional neighborhood health centers were established by Johnson, across the country. "It just so happened that SUR had gotten a master's in public health and was selected as the medical director and administrator." Under Sam's supervision and leadership, the health center grew to a sizable patient population.

PUBLIC HEALTH PURSUIT AND MPH DEGREE: 1965–1968
"Of all the forms of inequality, injustice in health care is the most shocking and inhumane."

MARTIN LUTHER KING JR.

KANSAS CITY: BACK TO SCHOOL ANNOUNCEMENT, 1965
My father sold his interest in the doctors' clinic, uprooted his life and his family's, and set his sights on his next career and the next frontier of public health. My father headed to the University of Michigan, MPH bound, as an incoming student. I remember the day my father announced he was going away to school in Michigan. My siblings and I, between the ages of thirteen to nine years of age, were attending different public schools, either bused or on foot. We listened, not fully comprehending what changes this might bring to our household, while fully understanding what it was to be a student. Rickey was attending his first year of junior high

school at Central, while I continued at Dunbar Elementary without my big brother for the first time. Rita had enrolled in an accelerated academic program at a different public school, mirroring her father's Talladega academic path.

Dr. Rodgers moved out of his comfortable three-story family home with all the conveniences into a graduate dormitory with a roommate. He flew home to Kansas City every two weeks to check on us. My mother was required to learn to drive and acquired her driver's license. Her brother, Richard—the Tuskegee Airman—taught her. My brother, at fifteen, was old enough to get his driving permit and eventually became our chauffeur when needed, at his pleasure of course. Rita and I baked homemade chocolate chip cookies every two weeks. We packed the cookies in a shoe box, wrapped it in Kraft paper (butter stains and all), and mailed it to Ann Arbor.

We transitioned for two years into a new lifestyle. Our family relocated to Ann Arbor, Michigan, the summer of 1966 to be together again as my father finished his studies. We all grew into our new roles and grew up a little more.

MPH graduation at the University of Michigan, Ann Arbor, Michigan, 1967

NEW BEGINNINGS AND BILL THE ROOMMATE, 1965

My father arrived at the University of Michigan in 1965 to nurture a longing, to take a childhood dream to another level—only he was no longer a child, but a fifty-year-old student, with all the attention that brings. When he arrived, he was placed on academic probation and assigned a roommate.

Bill was a young student in the MPH program, a long way from home. My dad, a fifty-year-old, African American southpaw from Alabama with WWII honors and a notable thirty-year medical career. Bill, a thirty-year-old Anglo-Saxon, only child from Oregon, with no army affiliation or long-term career experience.

The two were truly an odd couple, at least that was how it seemed. However, Bill was the perfect match for my father. They were both quiet, easy going, and laid back. My family was comforted knowing my father had a friend he could trust, enjoy, and mentor in this new academic environment.

We came to know and love Bill and added more chocolate chip cookies to our bi-weekly mailing. Bill had become family, and in the late 1960s, my father drove us to Oregon, where we were hosted by Bill and his lovely parents on the sky slopes of Mount Shasta in northern California.

SUR'S WORLDVIEW OF STUDENT LIFE

On January 2, 2021, I interviewed Jim Nunnelly and learned a different side of a well-known story.

In 1969, Jim was a young twenty-seven-year-old medical school administrator when he began his career at WMHC. Rita and I were fourteen and thirteen years old, respectively. Jim watched the Three R's grow up, and Rita would become Jim's colleague twenty years later.

"You know, Daddy would chuckle about being placed on probation when he arrived at UM," I said. "Did you know that, Jim?"

We laughed about that too, but it wasn't because he had been out of school for so long. It was because they didn't believe he could keep up," Jim shared.

"The difficulty was he had the information in his head, but he couldn't get it down fast enough on paper," Jim stated.

My father had years of practical experience. He had succeeded in developing unique programs that targeted specific public health needs long before he pursued an MPH. SUR had decades of accumulated knowledge that he wanted to practically implement. He could teach the teacher, and he did. He was an inventive, prolific thinker with an active mind and a rapid speech cadence. His challenge was to document this onslaught of ideas as rapidly as they occurred. SUR had decades of accumulated experience that he wanted to share.

UM assigned a foreign student who was learning the English language as his writing assistant. The student wrote as my father spoke from a wealth of knowledge about patient care philosophies. The student writer gained exposure to the American perspective and culture, providing a win-win situation for both.

"After that, he was unstoppable," Jim said.

I mused, "So he's dictating and she's writing?"

"There you go!" Jim remarked.

Having so much experiential knowledge, he was not very receptive to other people's thoughts. He had seen health care from many perspectives by then. "I believe Dr. Rodgers saw his mission in attending Michigan as two parts: partly to learn and partly to transform. During the application process when asked where he attended school, some had never heard of Talladega College, yet he had practiced all these years. The only credibility established was that he had completed his residency in Kansas City; but again, at a black institution they had reservations about. So, his credentials were a little weak as there was information that they could not find nor validate," Jim explained. "It was not that he was not believable, but he didn't fit the mold of the customary student they would normally recruit. "

Dr. Rodgers was the embodiment of someone who had conquered the world, gained experience, then returned to school. Following this realization, people were going back to school left and right, after having worked in all kinds of arrangements, but it was strictly because Dr. Rodgers did.

MICHIGAN SCHOOL OF PUBLIC HEALTH SCHOLARSHIPS, 1965–1967

Jim continued, "Your father had such an influence on the Michigan School of Public Health. After his arrival, they begin to expand scholarships to people who were qualified in ambulatory care. He believed that these were the people that should know about and receive these scholarships. In turn, Michigan provided the majority of these. I always say that Dr. Rodgers was so undervalued because his involvement went well beyond patient care. At the health center, they thought of him as just a doctor who saw poor patients. That angers me because he was so much more than that."

"Dr. Rodgers convinced the University of Michigan School of Public Health to begin giving scholarships to working people. At that time, the school was only giving scholarships to students in high school or students from other undergraduate institutions. He convinced them to go out and find people who were worthy of getting a degree. These online advanced degree opportunities are a direct result of his influence." The University of Michigan was the first school to offer them.

Being placed on academic probation was a temporary distraction. It said more about the world than I was willing to concede. I pictured my father as he was put through these paces. He was not deterred. In telling this story my father would extol a "you've got to be kidding" laugh and continued his mission and purpose. I was amused and saddened all at once. What my father knew for sure was that his ancestors had already come a mighty long way. SUR's uncle, Julian Paris Rodgers, finished undergraduate and law school at UM in 1915. He knew the history of the revered African American educational institutions, the courage it took to desegregate General Hospital No. 2. What everyone around him mirrored was a lack of knowledge of these institutions, otherwise known as ignorance.

My father made an indelible print on the School of Public Health at UM. Sadly, one of his takeaway experiences was of young black students he would see isolated on this predominately white campus. He would return to Kansas City with a dire wish that neither of his daughters would experience this isolation; thus, I enrolled at Spelman College, an HBCU.

Not only did my father make his mark at UM, but our family life also changed. We gladly became part of the Michigan journey that expanded our perspectives.

DETROIT MICHIGAN, 1967

My father's uncle settled in Detroit and raised a family after determining the South was not a safe place to make a life. Uncle Julian's son Horace would be instrumental in providing many details of our Detroit visits that I never knew as a child. I would interview Cousin Horace, now our family historian, multiple times during my writing process. He provided the name of the delicious fried shrimp restaurant, the taste I had never forgotten, and the names of many streets.

My father drove our blue station wagon, family and food in tow, from Kansas City to Detroit for occasional summer visits. We would drive by the infamous "Hitsville USA" Motown building at 2648 West Grand Boulevard, where hits and performing artists were made. As my father drove down West Grand, we screamed, "Where, where?" straining to see the Hitsville facility from the car. Much to our surprise, Hitsville was a simple residential dwelling.

From 1961 to 1971, Motown had 110 top-ten hits. Top artists during that time period included the Four Tops and Stevie Wonder. On our car journey to Detroit the Three R's would listen to and sing along with Motown hits such as the Supremes' 1964 release "Come See About Me" and Marvin Gaye's 1964 hit "How Sweet It Is to Be Loved by You." We knew every word of every song—lyrics that I have not forgotten even today, although I can't remember what I did last week. Our favorite artist? Stevie Wonder!

We could relate to Stevie Wonder, a teenager, famous no less, just two years older than my brother. Wonder's song "Fingertips," recorded in 1963 with its staccato finger-popping beats and the distinctive harmonica sounds, was unforgettable. Wonder was thirteen at the time and would go on to become an international performing artist success and civil rights activist.

We would spend time with the Detroit Rodgers branch of our family, enjoying our visits and making more memories. My father was an advocate for family get togethers, as he wanted his children to experience the family that had formed his values. As the Three R's played with our cousins, we ran up and down the street breathlessly until we came to an abrupt stop. My cousin, pointing to a house two doors away from her home, nonchalantly said, "Stevie Wonder lives right there." In 2021—fifty-four years later—as I interviewed Cousin Horace and daughter, we relived many memories of our summer visits. The prior generation was gone, but never their memories.

As we ended the call, my cousin reminisced, "We could hear Stevie Wonder play as he practiced on his back porch."

"If he keeps practicing, he'll be good!" Horace proclaimed.

We ended our call with tearful laughter.

THE DETROIT RIOTS: JULY 23, 1967

My father continued to fly home to Kansas City bi-weekly, even in our absence. In the summer of 1967, on one of our routine drives from Ann Arbor to Detroit's Metropolitan Airport, it became far from routine. Bill, our new big brother, offered to drive us to Detroit to pick up Dr. Rodgers. My mother welcomed Bill's offer, still an inexperienced interstate driver.

We set off to the airport traveling through the inner city of Detroit on the last leg of the journey when suddenly the traffic came to an abrupt stop on either Milford or Grant Boulevard. Reading along the way, I had not kept abreast of the scenery. The scene I awoke to was harrowing.

Our car was surrounded by rioters, looters, police, and small fires, in gridlock traffic. I witnessed looters throwing large objects through glass storefronts, returning with frozen turkeys then thrown into the back of postal trucks. In that moment, I realized the potential peril of being driven while black by a white driver. I wasn't sure who was most endangered, but I knew it wasn't good. I gripped my head between both hands and prayed for our safety. At age twelve, having already experienced the civil rights struggles in the south, I became an eyewitness to northern style racism and police brutality.

I would learn these facts later after our narrow escape. "The Detroit Riot of 1967 was a series of violent confrontations between residents of predominantly African American (AA) neighborhoods in Detroit and the city's police department. It began on July 23, 1967 and lasted five days. The riot resulted in the deaths of forty-three people, including thirty-three African Americans and ten whites. ("1967 Detroit Riots"- Causes, Facts & Police /Updated MAR 23, 2021). What I knew for sure, as my father explained, was the deeper causes of the riot were rooted in resentment, anger, and frustration among African Americans, resulting from centuries of racism, segregation, and lack of economic and educational opportunities.

We were delayed picking up my father but escaped unharmed. This incident would become my most impactful memory of that time. After 1967 following my father's graduation from UM, I did not visit Detroit again until our July 28, 2017, family reunion, years after my father's death.

Health and Transformation

"To be poor is really tough, to be sick is really tough; but to be both, there's nothing worse."

—DR. SAMUEL ULYSSES RODGERS

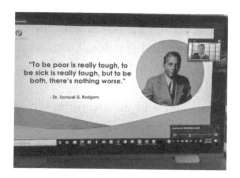

It was several years after the excitement of the 2018 gala when I took quiet time to sit and read every word of the beautifully prepared program—a keepsake from that night. It contained a timeline of event and program development at the health center that summed it up just right. What was missing was the "magic glue" created by the underlying character of special people and their missing pieces of the puzzle that would make it all complete.

In 1968, my father opened the fourth community health center, a first in the state of Missouri, in the 911 Michigan building of the Wayne Miner Housing Project. He then set about the most essential phase: the staffing of the center with all the right people. SUR routinely kept his finger on the pulse of who was doing what in the health care community. He would hire many young and experienced professionals in a most serendipitous way. He knew instinctively what would work. It was unconventional recruiting by instinct.

SUR proceeded with staffing the entire Wayne Miner Health Center (WMHC), strategically aligning personnel based on areas of need. He staffed without knowing precisely what each role would entail, and without developing specific tasks right away. SUR staffed the center with the best people he could find to accomplish his vision, his mission. Even today, all staffing is executed per Dr. Rodgers' vision.

My father was quiet and unassuming, but strategic. He would begin a conversation with a leading question while already knowing the answer.

SUR hired all board-certified physicians—not student doctors as some accused, an outstanding recruitment feat. SUR was like a magnet, drawing the best and brightest to contribute to his vision.

I recalled reading the book, *Good to Great: First Who, Then What* by Jim Collins. The book conveyed, "Those who build great organizations *first ensure* they have the right people on the bus, and the right people in the right seats, *then* they figure out how to take it someplace great." I doubt my father ever read this book, but he understood this concept deep in his bones. "They always think first about who, and then what." Dr. Rodgers was a student of human behavior. According to the book the good-to-great leaders understood that, " Great vision without great people is irrelevant."

Then sometimes people find you.

INTERVIEW WITH JOSEPH FRANCIS HARKINS IN LAWRENCE, KANSAS

Joe Harkins expressed instant delight when he received my call on January 9, 2021. Immediately without hesitation, he asked, "How's your brother Rickey and sister Rita?" I hesitated, surprised that he remembered our names, knowing fifty-three years had passed. I explained my brother passed away December 1998, one year before my father. "I didn't know…I'm so sorry. I admired your family. You all were so important to your dad, but of course you know that already."

Joe's history reached back before the official opening, when he was appointed as the first health center administrator (Information Systems /Business) of WMHC from 1968 to 1970. Harkins had been the administrator of the Cancer Research Center from 1964 to 1968 and resided in Columbia, Missouri. "The senior staff assembled at the health center loved your dad and were loyal to him." The Truman Hospital

(TH) Medical School, started in the early 1970s, joined with the old county hospital. Administrators desired to establish TH as the anchor of community health care. "To hell with that," my father had replied. WMHC existed precisely because Truman Hospital had failed to serve the community.

"Your dad was tough!"

Harkins first became aware of the evolution of the WMHC development through his local newspaper. He had spent four years in Columbia, Missouri, developing a cancer research center, and there appeared to be difficulties with opening WMHC. Joe had never met SUR but knew he had made a big career change to head up a new health center.

"I was young, looking for a challenge, and had successfully started a new health facility from scratch. I thought maybe Dr. Rodgers could use my help."

Joe phoned SUR and asked if they could meet, stating, "I'm interested in working for you." Because Dr. Rodgers was not interested in dealing with a stranger over the telephone, Joe scheduled an appointment and drove to Kansas City. They had a productive visit, asked questions of each other, and hit it off. In reflection, Joe was proud of what transpired in their first meeting. "He was a cautious guy and didn't immediately embrace me as a trusted friend."

THE WAR ON POVERTY

Health care for the poor was a big part of the War on Poverty. Organizations like Model Cities and the Health Education

Welfare (HEW) sponsored neighborhood health centers. SUR walked Joe through the boarded-up apartments. The complex was built like a prison, with a central infield court. Patterns of bullet holes from automatic rifles sprayed throughout rooms, where someone had opened the door and pulled the trigger. "It was just awful. I had several days of second thoughts," Joe said.

The staff was hired, three floors of the WMHC complex were rented, and SUR knew what he wanted to do. It made sense to Joe and the two men agreed to work together. "I returned home to Columbia, resigned from my job, packed up my family, and moved to Kansas City."

Joe's wife, a nurse, agreed and understood the importance of neighborhood health centers to inner city communities. It was a risky decision for the young couple with three small children, but they understood the significance of my father's mission. Years later, Joe was unable to disguise his admiration for my father. He knew SUR's heart and soul was in this project. If he was willing to make that kind of commitment it was worth the risk. Joe concluded that it was one of the best decisions he'd made in his life.

"In those days it wasn't easy for people from different races to form a bond. It was a tense time for race relations, but we were able to rise above that and get along just fine," Joe acknowledged. The two men committed to each other to make it work. No one had ever opened a health center before, and WMHC was one of the first built in the country.

Health centers were done under the auspices of Office of Economic Opportunity (OEO), as coordinated by the Kansas City Community Action Agency (CAA). Health care was considered a part of that strategy. CAAs were a network of local, private, nonprofit, and public agencies created through the Economic Opportunity Act of 1964, which aimed to alleviate poverty. (About Community Action)

Part of the OEO movement also embraced the Model Cities Initiative (1966–1972). Everything we did was within the framework of the War on Poverty as part of the civil rights movement, the nation's reaction following the 1960s riots. Opportunities were being created by Congress. "You simply had to have the ability to take advantage of what was available," Joe explained.

In November 1966, President Lyndon B. Johnson signed into law an act as a centerpiece to his Great Society program, which planned to relieve urban blight, poverty, and hardship in America's inner cities. The Model Cities Program decentralized decision making, reducing the federal government's role in local matters. This bottom-up approach to urban renewal placed responsibility in the hands of cities, planning commissions, and service providers. (Center for the Study of Federalism, 11/2/2018.)

The War on Poverty legislation introduced by President Johnson, during his State of the Union Address on January 8, 1964, was part of a larger legislative reform program, the Great Society Program, intended to end poverty in the US, affecting 20 percent of the population. Johnson identified societal failure as the cause of poverty, such as lack of education, medical care, and housing. (Britannica: War on Poverty, Aaron Cooley)

James Threat came to KC to run Model Cities. Threat was an unforgettable personality who made his presence known when he walked into any room. "He always made an entrance," Joe laughed. Threat, a brilliantly clever strategist, found additional streams of funding through HEW outside of the original OEO funds received by WMHC. In addition, Threat contended that if money was provided for WMHC, we should pursue funding for an additional health center in Kansas City. He was also instrumental in attracting key personnel with stellar resumes to WMHC. Harry Gumby, a retiring chief administrator at the Richards-Gebaur Air Force Base Hospital, became one such recruit.

PREPAID GROUP PRACTICES (PGPS) AND TRADITION PRACTICE

Joe's prior career experiences created an acknowledged personal bias concerning the design of health centers. He believed PGPs were the best medical delivery system that had ever been developed in this country. PGPs, the main type of HMO, could directly combine prepayment for health care with a comprehensive health care delivery system and professionals to supply the right mix of services.

The only organization of medical care occurred when patients were admitted to a hospital. Doctors couldn't care for patients outside of a hospital structure, as they traditionally managed separate medical records in solo practices. Joe's bias was based on medical care practices, built by the Kaiser Corporation during World War II in California. Joe was influenced by this model as the design of WMHC began. "We had the ambulatory care but were missing the hospital piece," Joe said.

The Neighborhood Health Center concept was developed as an alternative to health care for the poor that, in most cities, was built around secondhand hospitals that had been white hospitals first. A better hospital was then built for the white population. With such inherent bias, health care became "institutionalized segregation" by design that penetrated the whole practice of medicine. These values were reflected in the way health care organizations operated. It was the neighborhood health center revolution that targeted the real problem, which was fixable. "Our focus was to develop a neighborhood health center based primarily on the prepaid group practice model, minus the hospital piece," Joe explained.

Dr. Rita commented, "In the days of segregated Hospital Hill, poor people who received what's now called primary care didn't receive primary care at all."

"Care was received only in the emergency room," Joe recalled.

THE POWER BROKERS

GH2 in Kansas City was in terrible shape after years of neglect and underfunding. People had conflicting philosophies about how to correct these conditions, depending on who you were. There was a power structure in Kansas City composed of vice presidents, chairs of local associations, trusts and foundations, and the medical establishment. They respected SUR a great deal but offered a different solution.

Their vision was to solve the quality of health care for the poor by building a new, modern hospital to replace General Hospital. They had tremendous influence and support at City Hall and were proceeding in that direction. "Then along comes your dad with a grant to build WMHC. These were not compatible concepts."

WMHC was based on the concept of comprehensive ambulatory care (i.e., outpatient care) with the secondary emphasis on hospitalization. Their model was the traditional teaching hospital model, where patients were addressed as part of a teaching curriculum. These were not bad people, but people who proposed an elegant teaching hospital as the solution. "We ran into them—head on—like fullback linebackers," Joe said.

The power brokers could not understand why we were not cooperating. "Give us the money you've received for this health center, for our use in building our new hospital or temple. We had many knock down drag out arguments," Joe laughed.

"Our team had Sam Rodgers, who was not a world-famous cardiologist like Gray Diamond, nor a former full professor from a medical school. I was a young twenty-four-year-old, small-town white kid, who didn't know anything. We went up against them and didn't make any friends," Joe relished saying decades later. Joe relished in knowing he and my father had the better solution that prevails today at SURHC—the solution that sees people first with their surrounding life circumstances.

"Like David and Goliath?" I asked.

"Yes! And I loved it because I knew we had the better idea," Joe said.

Like David and Goliath, SUR and Joe's story was a lesson in courage, faith, and overcoming what seemed impossible.

The Health Center Opening

MEETING AND MENTORSHIP

Jim Nunnelly grew up at Wayne Miner Health Center (WMHC) experiencing many kismet-like opportunities through SUR, personally and professionally throughout his life.

Jim eventually became involved in community matters outside of WMHC. This was not viewed apart from the health center, but instead it was integral to my father's master plan for community transformation. As we began the interview, Jim described himself as SUR's best experiment. "There was something magical about SUR's credibility."

UNIVERSITY OF MISSOURI MEDICAL SCHOOL (COLUMBIA, MISSOURI)

In 1966, SUR visited with medical school officials with the sole purpose of bawling them out for inactive recruitment of black medical students. Jim knew medical school politics after having served as registrar of the medical school in the dean's office for four years, when he serendipitously met Dr. Samuel Rodgers. Jim reported there were approximately 500 medical students. "How many black people?" my father had asked.

Jim had recently completed the selection confirmation package of one hundred new medical students, when he was contacted by Governor Warren E. Hearnes. The governor requested that three new spots be made available in the upcoming class. Jim replied, firmly explaining the selections were finalized and complete.

On Thursday, SUR coincidentally wandered into Jim's office overhearing this exchange. SUR saw a diamond in the rough in Jim, knowing that WMHC could use a young professional who could match wits with the power elite, while thinking outside the box. By the end of the day, SUR had contacted Joe Harkins, the first health center administrator (1968–1969) to determine an affordable salary for Jim. The following Monday, SUR made a job offer to Jim to become an employee of WMHC.

JIM'S STUDENT LIFE

Jim Nunnelly attended University of Missouri from 1966 to 1969 on a full scholarship with assistance from the NAACP as an English major. It was a traumatic experience in the predominately white university environment. With a student population of approximately 17,000 white students, fewer than one hundred African American students were viewed as rule violators. Following graduation, Jim worked at a local grocery store where he would meet the wife of the dean of the University of Missouri Medical School, who recommended him to the Dean. In preparation for his interview, Jim surveyed passers-by in a medical building lobby, simply asking, "Do you know who your doctor is?" He shared his observations in the interview with the dean and was hired as the registrar of the medical school.

Initially, Jim disliked the path planned before him, seemingly against his will. "I wondered why Dr. Rodgers took so much interest in me." Jim learned from his mother years later, shortly before her death, that Dr. Rodgers visited with his parents in Columbia, Missouri, years ago. The knowledge of this meeting had never been shared with Jim by SUR or his parents, Mr. and Mrs. Nunnelly. Jim accepted the job offer at WMHC and moved his family to Kansas City with his parents' blessings, totally unaware.

In June of 1968, the staff moved into the vacated housing projects and Wayne Miner Health Center officially opened at 911 Michigan Avenue. Thirty staff members were on payroll.

"A big part of my job was to build the new health center. Dr. Rodgers was so proud of this health care facility that it literally became the physical manifestation of his vision to deliver a world class health care system that would become the first of its kind," Jim said.

As far as I can recall Jim Nunnelly was always there like family, and amazingly, he still is. "I drank from the well Dr. Rodgers dug," Jim said. "Now I'm very prepared and have made a difference." Jim would serve at the health center thirteen consecutive years (1969–1982) before returning in 1986. Jim was twenty-seven years old when he began his career with SUR.

HARRY GUMBY: CHIEF OF STAFF, INTERNAL AFFAIRS (1970–1975)

Harry Gumby (retired army) served as a sergeant in the US army for thirty years. He was retired and had decided he only wanted to work for two more years. He more than doubled that time, leaving the health center about five years later. Jim Nunnelly served as administrator of development, handling external affairs. Harry was the everyday administrator over internal affairs and daily operations of the health center. Jim and Harry shared the same space, each with a specific focus. Mr. Gumby was good for Jim, and they had a good relationship. My father, no surprise, chose this pairing. I remember Mr. Gumby as a quiet and effective behind-the-scenes operator; a good listener, calm and disciplined presence; an outstanding administrator. "Gumby helped with stabilizing the health center allowing Dr. Rodgers to go home early." Mr. Gumby had an "easy disposition," one in perfect alignment with my father's.

Of the current staff, Mr. Gumby was most likely the closest in age to my father, just seven years his junior. They had an unspoken understanding that comes from "the greatest generation" ethos as coined by journalist Tom Brokaw, having served their country in World War II. Jim knew very little about my father's army years but shared that my father had proudly shown him the gun he carried on his shoulder as he traveled across Italy during World War II. Jim Nunnelly, the other bookend, was an outgoing, gregarious, curious, and never-met-a-stranger personality. Jim was the "ear to the ground," a necessity in this ever-changing community, the person who checked in with the city and knew the politics and pulse of the neighborhood and health care community.

JAMES "JIM" THREAT: ASSISTANT CITY MANAGER (1968)

Jim Threat was known as "the operator." As a child I was fascinated and entertained by the presence of Mr. Threat. SUR covered all the bases by surrounding himself with the best and the brightest, whether they recognized that in themselves or not. Jim Threat was wily, good hearted, and could find the money to support good causes. He was knowledgeable about federal grants. Mr. Threat was excited, expressive, and fully engaged in whatever he chose to give his time to. Now as an adult I view Jim as a strategist, a Cornel West-like figure both brilliant and fiery. His enthusiasm and candor made my daddy laugh. His skills as a political operative gained my father's respect.

COMMUNITY AND PATIENT DIVERSITY

A large immigrant Vietnamese community near the health center was associated with nearby St. John's Catholic Church. Though described as subdued and soft spoken, Minh successfully guided hundreds of Vietnamese families to receive health care services, amid the language barriers.

Nunnelly met with the St. John's priest, and SURHC hired several Vietnamese high school students as staff interpreters to allay the language and cultural fears and to increase the success rate of treating this population of patients. Minh became an instrumental part of orienting a new immigrant culture to health care and the US. Minh met and married optometrist Dr. Lewis Manuel while employed at SURHC. Minh Manuel, a Vietnamese immigrant, became the first patient representative and interpreter employed at the health center, for more than thirty-five years.

OSTEOPATHIC SCHOOL

As a steppingstone to building a world-renowned reputation, SUR developed relationships with the adjacent neighboring osteopathic school found within blocks of the health center. He asked, "How can you have a school across the street and not engage with them?" A medically trained practitioner seeing any value in associating with an osteopath was considered a crazy risk in those days, as osteopaths were and are still viewed by many as "quacks" lacking true medical training.

Rita explained, "There were osteopathic residents and attending level instructors who agreed to come to SURHC and provide services once a week." Rita viewed this relationship as one of her accomplishments as the medical director. This relationship with SURHC provided a rich opportunity for the osteopathic training program by providing residents with exposure to patient care within the community.

SATURDAYS WITH THE RODGERS FAMILY

My father made the best use of his time, attending to his professional and family life—a seamless proposition. Thoughts of the health center must have been ever present.

In 1969, SUR was building a new reality based on a vision, brick by brick and person by person. His gift was that he made you feel like the center of his attention in that moment, and you were. My family had his undivided attention always. We understood he had a vision and a dream to fulfill. He considered fatherhood as a primary purpose and staff mentorship as a secondary professional goal in carrying out the dream. He adeptly crossed, not blurred, the two. It was common to have various health center staff at our home on Saturday afternoons in a one-on one with our father in the family den.

Jim Nunnelly was a regular on Saturdays, as my father would use these sessions to review the prior week and plan the next. "I came to look forward to these Saturday sessions," Jim said. "Mrs. Rodgers would prepare hamburgers with sauteed onions on top" for Dr. Rodgers. No one refused a meal at our home. My mother was an excellent cook, and every burner on our four-burner stove was always on overdrive. My parents fed everyone and there was always more than enough to go around.

James Threat, Kansas City's assistant city manager, would visit on Sundays. Jim Threat and Daddy would go back and forth discussing and debating concepts and approaches over prime rib, wild rice, and green bean dinners that ended with homemade apple pie. Mr. Threat's conversation was peppered with the latest local politics, intermingled with rave reviews for my mother based on his last mouthful of food. Jim Threat was brilliant, outspoken, and passionate about the causes he supported. A bigger-than-life public personality and a precursor to a Cornel West-type persona.

Amid these "summit sessions" were the constant ramblings of the pre-teen Three R's on our way to the next thing.

"Your mother loved to cook, and I would be her Saturday taster, although she never gave me a full meal."

Jim had no way of knowing that Saturdays were off limits in our house for three square meals, definitely the norm throughout the week. Saturdays were reserved for hamburgers, chili dogs, chili, and spaghetti. He'd just always been there on the wrong day.

In 1968, Jim at twenty-four was just beginning his professional career. He knew of Clara's stellar reputation in nursing and recruited only the best. What they had in common were willing spirits, even temperaments, honest character, and trust in SUR. What all three had in common was a steely determination to improve the conditions of a people and community they knew all too well.

NEVER A DULL MOMENT

I first called Ms. Clara Maddox for a re-introduction after nearly twenty years of being out of touch. I explained that I was writing my father's memoir, and with no hesitation, Clara agreed to participate. Within minutes of the first contact call, Clara shared a funny story about my father, and we ended the call with laughter. These instantaneously shared stories became the norm, and I invited my sister Rita to join each Zoom interview so as not to miss these captivating stories. "You just have to be there to hear it in person," I would say, and she never missed a single call.

Clara Maddox was a long-term SURHC employee. She began her employment in 1969 and worked with my father for twenty-five years, launching many novel programs during her tenure and retiring in 1994. Ms. Maddox held two positions at the health center: community health director and director of Project High Blood.

I began, "How did you meet my father and start working at the health center?"

"Dr. Rodgers was my OB-GYN. I remember when he started delivering babies, at the first doctors' clinic located on Brooklyn. It was their first office, and two of my children were born there." When her third child was born, Dr. Rodgers had moved to the newly constructed doctors' clinic. She of course remembered Drs. Carl Peterson, W. R. Peterson, and Starks Williams. "I was working for visiting nurses and had stopped at a hamburger place. Dr. Rodgers saw me, walked in, and said, 'Listen, I'm starting this new health center, and I need you to come to work for me.'"

"Oh really? Doing what?" Clara had responded.

"Doing what you're doing right now."

"Well, how's that going to work?"

"Well, that will be up to you," Dr. Rodgers had said.

"Ok," Clara had replied.

"Well, when can you start?" he had asked.

"I'll give notice, and I'll be down there soon."

Clara had worked three years in her current job at the Veteran's Administration (VA) Hospital but had grown tired of the late-night hours. "I ran into Dr. Rodgers several days later, and his offer of regular working hours was appealing. And that's the way I started."

"In 1969 we began by opening multiple community centers on 12th Street, one on the west side, one on the east side, where people could get blood pressure checks and wait on transportation to the health center. We decided in 1970 that this set up wasn't working and started a home health care program where people could be cared for in their homes. This proved to be the solution that worked."

Clara was unique among the interviewees. She had knowledge of and personal experience with several well-known Kansas City institutions that were key milestones in my parents' life story and held a special place in our hearts.

"Are you familiar with Queen of the World (QOTW) hospital?" I asked. "Yes, that's where all my children were born. It's on 23rd Street right before you get to Indiana Street." I shared QOTW was also where Rita and I were born. Ms. Maddox remembered QOTW was run by Catholic sisters. Clara had also attended Lincoln High School just like my mother, the only high school available to blacks at the time.

We would be entertained throughout Clara's interview, unaware but not surprised by our father's unorthodox approaches. SUR provided unique growth opportunities to many who were overlooked due to race and gender. Beyond professional excellence, SUR heavily considered people's character.

A New Day

My father was a problem solver who viewed people and their circumstances through the keen eyes of compassion and realism. What improved their surrounding physical circumstances was pivotal in improving the quality of their lives. Innovation dwells in the creative mind of one who truly seeks a solution. Moral strength is power. While some proceed with caution, my father proceeded with courage to create a more humane approach to patient care.

In 1971, the Wayne Miner Health Center (WHMC) moved to 825 Euclid Avenue, to a forty-seven-thousand-square-foot facility designed specifically for health care services directly across the street from the former WMHC projects. Their compassionate health care approach attracted five thousand new patients.

9th & Euclid Street Signage

A NEW VISION IN HEALTH CARE DELIVERY

Dr. Rodgers envisioned, then conceptually designed, every detail of the new health center with the goal of removing any physical, mental, financial, socio-economic, class, or language barriers.

Jim explained, "He thought about the physical workflow, the patients' first encounter as they entered the lobby, who would greet them, where and how they would get to their specified appointments, how long they would wait, and how they would travel to and from the facility. Most importantly, how they would afford their care and pay for the prescribed medications."

NAVIGATION

The philosophy of navigation through the health care system was borne and implemented at the Sam Rodgers Health Center by Dr. Rodgers. It involved viewing patients as humanly valued and went well beyond way-finding signage systems, focusing on the human element of how a patient was addressed within a health care system. Navigation focused on the patients' comfort level and trust of the health care system, too often ignored.

Based on my father's vision, there would be no obstacle, whether imagined or actualized, to receiving quality health care by this new patient population. Many reasons existed based on the racist mistreatment of African Americans throughout the history of this country for them to be distrustful of a system that had consistently taken advantage of and excluded their health care needs and humanity. Dr. Rodgers left no stone unturned in his detailed consideration of patient deterrents.

UNIFORMS

The traditional uniformed practice of "doctors and medical staff in white coats" was eliminated as it created an unapproachability issue for this population of patients. My father wanted to eliminate any fear or hesitation for the patients, who were on the receiving side of health care. The RNs wore gold and the LPNs wore turquoise jackets, to distinguish status, over their natural clothes. Jim added, "The only medical practitioners allowed to wear 'white waiter-style jackets' were dentists."

In 1974, I began my studies at Kansas State University's School of Architecture. I remember witnessing this approach firsthand while touring the new health center with my father, as an architectural design student. Arriving in the large but welcoming lobby space, it became clear that your presence would not be overlooked as a patient waiting to be called. Per my father's vision, a patient would be acknowledged as having arrived and given a specific appointment time. This unique welcome said at once, "You matter here." Dr. Rodgers understood that acknowledging the patient from the beginning to the end of the medical visit establishes your level of respect for their humanity.

EYE SEE YOU

Few details were overlooked in the design of the health center. Virtually every interior space had glass windows, not curtains. Jim later described, "You could see everything and everybody. Patients were not left in enclosed offices or hidden behind drawn curtains where they could be forgotten and overlooked for hours, as they waited for care."

As if reading his mind, I asked, "Why would a patient trust you one step further with their care if they were not greeted with kindness and respect?"

Turning to face me, he responded with a knowing look and smile. He knew I understood, and with no additional explanation, we continued our tour.

As we continued through the lobby, I noticed a large piece of equipment pushed against the wall—impossible to miss. The visibility of this monstrosity was its ultimate downfall. It alarmed when you stepped on the weighing platform, announcing your use. My father's latest well-intentioned addition was short-lived.

My father was described as "radical" concerning the epidemic of obesity because of the predictability that led to, and threatened, other states of disease (i.e., heart disease, hypertension, diabetes). A typical weighing scale in a medical practice did not go beyond a measuring weight of three hundred pounds. He ordered and installed a scale that would accommodate and records weights of up to five hundred pounds.

I hadn't known—but was not surprised to hear—my father was described as an "obesity radical." I had childhood memories of my father hospitalizing pregnant patients who had exceeded recommended weight expectations in their early trimesters. Before the advent of insurance company takeover of health care; this was permissible as a doctor in the best interests of the patient.

Accompanying my parents to formal functions, the Three R's could always count on the "How's your weight?" question, as guests approached our table. My father's query was applied across the board as applicable, with no malintent. It sprang from a well of concern on his part. The response was never one of surprise or negativity.

"Oh, Dr. Rodgers, you know how it is. I'm working on it!"

My father's not-so-subtle weight inquiries were acceptable to his patients. It was a small price to pay, as he had proven his value with the most important gift of all: the possibility of giving birth.

My father was adored by throngs of patients under his care as a private practitioner. He and his medical partners were rockstars and trailblazers long before he envisioned public health and the health center. Due to segregation and the rarity of African American board-certified medical practitioners, he was credited with delivering many of the black children in Kansas City.

Many patients, having dealt with infertility issues, were forever grateful that under Dr. Rodgers' care they eventually became parents. My father played an important role and was present in many of their most life-shattering or memorable moments. The faith-filled times were never forgotten by the patients, so at formal functions our table was met with rounds of adoring patients, anxious to thank and express their joy regardless of how many years had passed. These frequent visitations during these social events were a welcome break from the routine monotony after thirty plus years of attendance. My father, above all, was an astute observer of people and their behavior. I imagine they never forgot how God answered prayers using medically skilled people eager to serve as a conduit for his miracles.

SPECIAL NEEDS

Jim continued, "We made provisions for special needs." The health center was one of few professional facilities in the

1970s that provided ramps for wheelchair patients long before the advent of the American Disabilities Act (ADA). "The real paradigm shift that Dr. Rodgers made was that you were not really taking care of this patient population unless you were meeting them where they were."

"Actions speak louder than words" continued to define my father's approach to change, problem solving, and acceptance by others. Few people questioned his motives, which were proven over time. If you doubted his sincerity, you had only to watch. Change comes only with consensus, and consensus comes only with trust.

Manifest Excellence

1980 JOINT COMMISSION ACCREDITATION
The Joint Commission was an organization that certified the credibility of hospitals for insurance payments and later would include Ambulatory Care Accreditation. "They were the IRS in medical care," as Jim explained. Ambulatory care was medical care provided on an outpatient basis, with no plan to stay beyond the visit duration. In the early 1980s, hospitals began to provide ambulatory care and struggled with the physical part. Most community health centers wouldn't touch it. It was fortuitous that Dr. Rodgers was supportive of ambulatory care and had already implemented this service at WMHC.

My father was most often on the leading edge of medical initiatives. He walked where most feared to tread and when it was not always popular. This boldness caused no personal stress but created uneasiness in others whose motives were not as pure.

In 2022, Jim Nunnelly would again share his story as an eyewitness to these events.

SUR was a physician who truly cared about the care patients received, distinguishing him from most. Jim's role was to cultivate community acceptance, an acceptance often questioned. "What is your standard of care?" asked the medical community. Although WMHC was hiring and expanding, accreditation became increasingly important to SUR. WMHC had been incorrectly criticized for hiring physicians viewed as insufficient. The notion of accreditation had applied solely to hospitals. Accreditation was not a requirement for ambulatory care facilities or medical practices. No community health center had ever attained this distinction for care.

For decades, SUR had been critical of the quality of health care provided in most inner-city communities; specifically of the substandard care provided at Kansas City's GH2. Other health centers were predominately managed by businesspeople and politicians. Under SUR's leadership, SURHC was growing the ambulatory care practice, providing patient transportation, hiring certified records personnel, and retaining registered certified nurses on staff.

SUR was willing take the risk of opening the center to scrutiny because much was at stake, including his reputation. His immediate goal was to quiet the naysayers. His goal was to establish quality health care as the cornerstone for future community development and housing. "If you let the community die around you it will begin to impact your ability to deliver health care. Echoing SUR's philosophy Jim said, " If we can succeed with at least one essential element (i.e., health care) then we have a chance to transform this community."

SUR assigned Jim to the task of organizing this effort.

"I believe SUR was most proud of me the day he assigned me the task of attaining national accreditation for the health center," Jim reminisced.

The accreditation process was tedious, involving the on-site review of open records by the outside accreditation team. The review team stayed longer than the normal one-week period, sending ten physicians to participate in the review. SURHC would be the first health center to undergo this process, making history. Jim described my father as a little edgy. "Are we ready?" he would ask daily, meeting with Jim hourly throughout the day.

The entire SURHC staff attended the accreditation exit inter-view to learn the results. SUR was notably uneasy, awaiting their final words. They revealed they stayed for an extended period, out of disbelief in the quality assurance already in place. An accreditation team member who observed both care and credentialing records remarked "no one in ambu-latory care had achieved this."

An examining physician remarked, "Dr. Rodgers, we have never been so pleasantly surprised because you embody what we teach our doctors to do when they go into the world."

My father was able to actualize the written medical liter-ature and put it into practice. He broke through barriers at a level no one expected and, in many ways, helped save the reputation of the medical health care movement. Only one of twelve health centers at the time, SUR's leadership became the guideposts that set health centers apart, rendering them credible and reputable. Visitors arrived at SURHC from across the country and around the world seeking to learn from SUR.

The WMHC became the first center in Missouri to become accredited by the Joint Commission of Hospitals (JCOH), providing new home-health services to home-bound patients.

Following the successful landmark accreditation, Jim became the first African American recruited as a member of the official site assessment tour team. Jim's ten-year experience as an accreditation team member would open new doors, taking him around the world to Paris, Germany, and Puerto Rico.

A WELL-WATERED SPROUT

It was a memorable five-year period from 1980 to 1985. While WMHC celebrated an accreditation milestone, our family rooted for, then celebrated, Dr. Rita's completion of medical school, then residency in 1985. We also rooted for, then celebrated the life of our mother.

My mother lived to see the culmination of my parents' shared dreams and joint sacrifices at SURHC. Jim Nunnelly left after thirteen years of service and returned one year following my mother's death. The highs and lows of life are random and none of us gets to choose the order, time, or place. My father somehow dealt with it all in a similar place and time.

The joy and satisfaction of a daughter who follows in your footsteps while not knowing how to take your next step after the loss of your spouse and best friend. Joy of all sorts can collide or coincide with grief, or go unnoticed.

Life goes on, and there is satisfaction in knowing the seeds of the future are already planted. They sprout and bloom, watered with time. My parents' labor would continue to bear good fruit in our family and community just as they intended.

Rita fulfilled her calling shown early in life. As I watched her walk across the stage to receive her medical diploma, I remembered that December 25, 1960, Christmas day long ago. In 1982, my sister graduated from St. Louis University Medical School (1978–1982) and completed her residency from 1982 to1985. This period became one of our proudest yet saddest time of our lives.

MOTHER'S DEATH, 1985

My mother died, at what I now consider the young age of sixty-four. I have now surpassed her in living age. She has been gone now far longer than she was in our lives, yet the pain never subsides. It was the hole in our lives that never closed. She was the sparkle and the love that lit up our entire home and life. None of us were prepared for this. It was not a sudden death, but a prolonged death due to colon cancer in the days before the advent of the diagnostic testing available today.

Rickey had chosen a career in law enforcement, Rita was amid her Houston medical residency, and I climbed the corporate ladder far away in New York. My mother was the heartbeat of our lives and so many others. Her death taught me many things; among them was to limit the misused refrain of, "Oh, things will get better with time."

My father's life would never be the same, but we all continued—because we had to. His bride and best friend of forty-one years was gone. Following her death, my girlfriends would comment on the notable loss of vibrancy in our home. Instead, my mother bequeathed us with a house full of love for each other.

Home on Quincy, Mom and Dad

Sometimes life presents opportunities that are strangely incomprehensible in the moment. The year my mother died, I, living in New York at the time, returned to Kansas City for minor surgery. I enjoyed eight to ten weeks of recovery, which spanned Thanksgiving, Christmas, and New Year's, to spend with my parents in recuperation. These holidays would be the last with my mother. I recalled standing in the doorway of my childhood bedroom, waving what seemed like a slow-motion goodbye to my bed-ridden, mother, knowing this would be our last. I waved, turned slowly, walked away, and returned. She knew too.

My mother had positively influenced so many lives: her closest and younger sister Barbara, neighbors, club members, the childhood friends of the Three R's, and even my father's patients and colleagues.

"Hello, may I speak with your mother?" a distressed patient calling our home would say. The caller was requesting my mother because they preferred to speak with her prior to speaking with their OB-GYN, Dr. Rodgers.

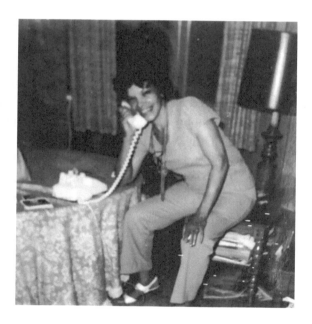

Home on Quincy, Mom

Our family lived a rich life of travel by car, train, or RV, survived all the normal childhood maladies of chicken pox, measles, mumps, and even kidnapping attempts. My father had developed an interest in RVs, and our quality of travel was upgraded as we traversed the country in this thirty-five-foot-home on wheels. My mother had been by my father's side during his journey of hospital desegregation and health center triumph.

As the Three R's grew into adulthood, we enjoyed our parents' company and would occasionally enjoy an evening of jazz together at Hallmarks Crown Center Hotel. My brother, a music lover, had found a friend and phenomenal voice in Oleta Adams. As a family we would listen for hours, mesmerized by her powerful voice and performance, as she crooned some of my parents' requested tunes. My father had a favorite song he would dedicate to my mother.

On the day of my mother's funeral, there was not a dry eye nor surface not covered with flowers. The chapel was standing room only; the lobby overflowed. It would be the first time I ever saw my father wipe tears from his eyes. From the hidden organ area at the front of the chapel you heard—but could not see—Oleta Adams sing "My Funny Valentine" in honor of my mother. Our hearts were laden with sadness, and time stood still. The song never leaves my mind.

The Renaming

My father gave new meaning to the term "underestimated," which he proved to be in many ways. Was this his fatal flaw— or did it instead become the flaw of others who presumed this? To assume SUR was arrogant based on his achievements would be a grave miscalculation, by any negotiator sitting across the table. My father never viewed his accomplishments as anything extraordinary. His commitment was something he was bound and determined to do, simply because it was right. This most disarming characteristic was mistaken many times as weakness.

1988 MILESTONES:

In 1988, the Wayne Miner Health Center (WMHC) celebrated twenty years of patient care and continued to lead the way in establishing essential health care programs. After two decades in operation, the Wayne Miner Health Center was renamed Samuel U. Rodgers Health Center (SURHC).

1988 renaming celebration at WMHC/SURHC

1988 downtown KC celebrates renaming

THE RENAMING

Jim Nunnelly spearheaded the renaming effort, although SUR was not a proponent. SUR avoided distractions from the true mission of the center or self-promotion. Jim's research indicated that fifty years had passed since anything was named after an African American in Kansas City health care. He remembered SUR's commitment in writing the history of GH2 for the *JNMA*, thus honoring the dedicated physicians who worked toward health care reform. These memories were Jim's motivation that SUR should be honored as well. SUR would not be Jim's only challenge.

A small group of black WWI veterans met monthly at the American Legion. Jim decided to attend to introduce the idea of the name change and caught hell from the veterans, receiving a history lesson that he would never forget. "This brave nineteen-year-old WWI soldier (Wayne Miner) served with honor, saving our lives; that's why we've named so many things in his honor," veterans countered.

Disappointed, Jim was reminded of my father's actions in the early days. "What should we call it?" someone had asked.

My father had replied, "If the center is going to be in the Wayne Miner projects, let the name remain. If it's going to be for the people, it should carry the people's name. "

Jim shared this story and others about SUR's years of dedicated service in WWII as a medic. This proved to be the turning point that defused the veterans' opposition and created mutual respect. "We educated each other—a priceless moment," Jim said.

Jim returned to SUR to report the backlash. "And why are you doing this?" my father asked again.

"Because health care is important for my generation too!"

SUR never brought it up again. With my father all things were done for the right reasons. SUR's leadership had been essential to the success of the center and its program offerings. The secret renaming process took two years, and in 1988 became a reality.

The basis for the right reason was always to improve the health and general well-being of individuals regardless of their ability to pay. Programs were developed to address internal organization opportunities, along with external community, national, and world issues.

A disciplined approach was needed internally to facilitate and support these programs through the development of health center guidelines.

Operational structure was critical to the success of any new organization, and often a point of criticism. My father had low tolerance for disorder of any type that would derail the center's ability to deliver world-class health care. SUR had the ability to quickly assess situations and the urgency to address them head on. This was why SUR hired Harry Gumby, a retired army sergeant, to create procedural guidelines for practices currently implemented and those on the drawing board. Harry brought effective practices from the military, such as the use of physician assistants (PAs) to SURHC. SUR hired the first PA outside of the army, marking the early acceptance of nurse practitioners. SURHC became the first ambulatory care facility to receive accreditation in the US.

AIDS PROGRAM: (C. MADDOX)

In 1988, WMHC established HIV counseling and testing services just as the AIDS pandemic swept across the country in the 1980s and early 1990s, Clara said. She described this experience as one of the most difficult things she had undertaken. Many young people were dying through no fault of their own. "They were dealing with issues that the community was not accepting of. It took time, community education, and easing of feelings. We had some serious soul searching to do."

RADIO SHOW (KPRS)

To foster community education, WMHC created a health news program "Highlights on Health" on KPRT 1590 a.m. Gospel radio. Clara proudly said, "This radio show was the first completely health related one in the country." Clara did the KPRS weekly radio program for ten to eleven years and relayed one of her most memorable stories.

A lady called in to report she had seen a doctor and her blood pressure was sky high. The caller said, "I'm listening to you tell people to get treated, but I can't afford the medicine." Dr. Rodgers intervened, telling the caller, "I'm going to take your name (off air), and by the time I get from here to the health center, I want you there." Dr. Rodgers addressed the caller's medical needs when they met at the center.

Dr. Rodgers' main concern was nobody who needed medicine left without it. If a prescription was written, he was adamant it needed to be filled. He ruffled many feathers of folks trying to collect a dollar from someone they thought had money.

A group at the Lansing State Prison listened to the radio program every week. Dr. Rodgers and Clara visited the prison several times. When they arrived at Lansing, they were asked to leave everything in a folder outside of the prison, in spite of my mother's recommendation to leave their ID at home. Once inside the prison they were met by two hundred young men, none of them over thirty.

The prisoners simply asked questions during the first visit, while the second SURHC visit addressed specific concerns about high blood pressure and diabetes. Clara explained the level of prison care appeared non-existent. Visitors were allowed in the same room only to talk; no touching allowed.

"It was sad to see so many young men—mostly black—whose main concern was health." The SURHC team phoned Kansas legislators and task force members to voice their concerns, but never learned directly if the concerns were addressed. Clara reported that Lansing Prison now has a nurse available once or twice a week and a hospital.

MATERNAL AND INFANT MORTALITY

The second area dear to our father's heart was prenatal and maternal /child infant mortality. Clara explained these focus areas were integrated in every health care initiative undertaken. A new prenatal program was opened to improve access to care for pregnant women. My father knew that poor patient-provider interaction for minorities was directly linked to disparities in health care.

"What is the infant and maternal mortality rate?" SUR would constantly ask. These measurements were both reflections of how successfully a woman's health was checked before, during, and after a pregnancy. "Did you follow through?" SUR would question. By that, he meant, had there been a continuum of patient health care along the way? High rates of both were a sign that you had not followed through medically.

Rita added, "I believe my father's effort was to ensure that we either provided the services to pregnant women, or they received pre-natal care. The only way you could deal with the horror of African American mothers dying at three to four times the rate of non-Hispanic white mothers is to make sure black women had access to medical care." Dr. Rita had recently presented weeks ago that there are "43.5 per 100,000 black infant deaths" as compared to "12.7 per 100,000 white infants"—an alarming statistic in this country, after all these years. (CAP Report 2/1/2018—Exploring African Americans' High Maternal and Infant Death Rates, Christina Novoa & Jamila Taylor). Clara wondered if these statistics were a result of fewer African American OB-GYNs. "Yes, and if you compare the death rate of a white physician taking care of a black woman versus a black physician taking care of a black woman, the death rate under the care of a black physician is half as much." We discussed inherent bias and issues with white practitioners who may not be hearing what the black patient is communicating.

Black babies are more likely to survive when cared for by black doctors. "Cumulative disadvantage throughout the life course is putting black and indigenous working people (and their babies) at greater risk for adverse outcomes," said University of Minnesota reproductive health equity researcher Rachel Hardeman. (USA Today, Nada Hassanein, 2021)

Clara concluded we must enroll more young people in medical and nursing schools. "If African Americans represent 13 percent of the general population, we certainly don't represent 13 percent of physicians," Rita said.

SURHC ANNUAL HEALTH FAIR: C. MADDOX

Around the time the AIDs program was beginning, SURHC decided to organize an annual health fair. It was a year-round planning effort, as Clara simultaneously built relationships with the American Heart Association and the Cancer and Lung National Association.

Attendees could receive mammograms, pap smears, eye exams, and childhood vaccinations. "You could practically receive a complete physical on health fair day. It was there, and it was free." Many of the attendees would become patients at the health center.

I observed, "Clara, SURHC was in the vanguard of offering programs that most medical organizations did not. How?"

"Well, I was the only one crazy enough to try. Your dad would propose a new idea and ask, 'Clara, what do you think?'"

"And you just kept rolling," I said.

"Yes," Clara said with a smile.

1989 TRIPS TO THE HILL (WASHINGTON, DC)

Rita and Clara recalled making annual multiple trips to "the Hill" with others to lobby for funding, presenting the case for the health center. I was more of an observer than anything, Rita said. The SURHC team traveled to Jackson, Mississippi, to get money and received funding from federal, city, and county governments, including universities. "We traveled to a lot of places and got blessed," Clara added.

On one such Washington visit, Dr. Rodgers and Clara Maddox met with a young infectious disease doctor—described as a tough talker—who was new to the world of funding. "Now I don't know where this fella is from, but you go and see what he's talking about. I will refrain from breaking bread with Fauci tonight, and we'll deal with what comes tomorrow." My father retired early that evening, sending Clara to dine with Fauci. That was their first meeting with Dr. Anthony Fauci.

"Well, did you get the money?" Dr. Rita asked.

"Of course," said Clara.

I knew many things for sure about my father. He was a man of few words like his father, Dr. Gordon A. Rodgers. He said what he meant, and he meant what he said. I smiled as I listened to this story because I knew above all my father cared about the disenfranchised, with all his heart and soul.

SUR was so committed to this mission, that his ultimate contribution was health care and community reform. He had little tolerance, patience, or understanding of anything or anybody that stood in the way of funding this cause; and that was the way it was. He was much more than a doctor.

Like Father, like Daughter

On December 19, 2020, it was my pleasure to jointly interview two alumni of the Samuel U. Rodgers Health Center (SURHC), Jim Nunnelly and Rita Rodgers Stanley. Their insights, observations, and keen recollections have supplied more memories than I could ever have expected. I would conduct a total of six interviews with the two, now friends with one another.

Dr. Rita Rodgers Stanley received her MD from St. Louis University in 1982. In 1985, she completed a residency in internal medicine at the University of Texas Health Science Center in Houston. Rita's four-year medical school education was paid for by the federal government through the Public Health Service Fulfillment Program, in exchange for four years of service in an underserved area. From 1985 to 1987, following residency, Dr. Rodgers Stanley worked as a physician for the Texas Department of Corrections, and from 1987 to 1989 was employed by the MacGregor Medical Association, Houston. Her last two years (1989–1991) were fulfilled at SURHC as a staff internist.

Rita explained, "In 1989, I returned to Kansas City to work at the health center. One, I always wanted to work with my father, and two, I still had two years left of my public health service obligation to fulfill." Interestingly, Rita found that treating patients at the health center was not unlike treating prisoners, described as an awesome experience. "Like indigent patients, the prisoners shared the challenge of access to decent health care and filed numerous lawsuits against the state of Texas alleging lack of care—and eventually won. TDC began setting up a system of care, much like the health centers. The only difference was my patients were incarcerated."

Two years after her arrival, Dr. Rita became medical director at SURHC from 1991 to 1994, a role she cherished.

Dr. Rita Rodgers Stanley named medical director

Uncertain of her new role as medical director, Dr. Rita explained the beauty of the FQHC. "Because we received millions of government dollars, there were detailed expectations around clinical care, more structure than in private practice, which I liked. It held us accountable for providing good care."

The Federally Qualified Health Center (FQHC) organization supplied structure and a framework that was particularly helpful to young physicians and public health administrators.

"I loved being medical director," my sister exclaimed. I could feel her spirit come alive, as she remembered past experiences. Her position involved working with providers as an advocate to ensure they were heard and were equipped to provide what was expected of them. It also required trips to Washington, DC, where she would meet women and men whose admiration for our father was palpable.

Rita especially recalled meeting a physician's assistant/nurse from Maine, who voiced a genuine interest to come and practice at the center. "I'll never forget her because—*wow*—she did just that." Dr. Rita was in the position to influence other professionals to join and experience an FQHC at a renowned health center, gaining an opportunity to work with Dr. Samuel Rodgers. SURHC had also fostered a strong relationship with the osteopathic school, enabling osteopathic residents and attendings to provide their services. "I was able to attract professionals for this moment-in-time opportunity, although their intent was never to stay."

THE ACORN THAT FALLS FROM THE TREE

There were so many similarities between the two: demeanor, temperament, and a heart of compassion. Dr. Rita was indeed her father's daughter in so many ways. I wondered if either ever saw themselves in each other. I could see it always. My sister exudes a quiet confidence and is capable, extremely intelligent, caring, and compassionate, a creative and visionary thinker. She was the neighborhood peacemaker and consoler if anyone's feelings were hurt during games of hide and go seek. I—not as diplomatic—was her protector at nursery school, ensuring she got her turn to ride the tricycle, continuously dominated by the rough and tumble boys. This was our first lesson in equal opportunity. We learned early on from our parents never to look down on anyone, display arrogance, or participate in name calling. These actions, if tried, were virtual misdemeanors in our home. All people are created equal—from those who delivered services to our home to those considered colleagues of our father.

My father's love for his family was never in question, nor our love for him. "You should be proud," Jim said. "You all were so blessed to have a father who was for you from the beginning, which gave you such a head start. His insight that came from the funky facts. I know that I personally owe him everything."

128th Anniversary Rodgers Chapel Celebration -
Wetumpka, Alabama

MENTORING

My father, either through natural tendencies or nurturing
qualities as an administrator and humanitarian, attracted
young physicians and professionals, many of whom saw him
as the fatherly presence they may have never had. He took
them under his wing, he cared. It was not surprising that
the sudden presence of my sister had an unpredicted effect
on those who considered themselves "SUR mentees." Rita
was well educated, professionally experienced, credentialed,
and board certified, not imposing or intimidating in the
least. More importantly she was biologically someone they
could never be: SUR's daughter. It is fair to venture that
these mentees experienced a loss of proximity to my father,
which may have been more imagined than real.

Rita was featured in a *Kansas City Star* newspaper article entitled "Doctor Sees Reality of Poor Daily." As a

third-generation physician in the Rodgers clan, this was nothing new. The article captured Dr. Rodgers seemingly "in motion," a photograph taken in an exam room with a patient. She was seated wearing a stethoscope around her neck, flipping through a patient chart that rested in her lap. Her head tilted toward the patient in a quizzical and concerned manner, her left hand the dominant page-turning hand. "Dr. Rita" was a "southpaw," just like her father. (Kansas City Star. "Doctor sees reality of poor daily." A-18, September 2, 1990)

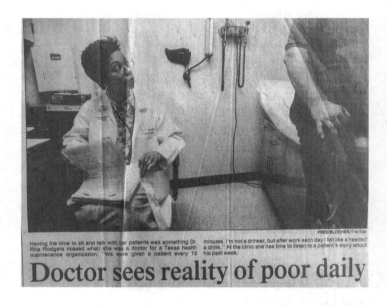

FRED BLOCHER/The Star

Having the time to sit and talk with her patients was something Dr. Rita Rodgers missed when she was a doctor for a Texas health maintenance organization. "We were given a patient every 15 minutes. I'm not a drinker, but after work each day I felt like a needed a drink." At the clinic she has time to listen to a patient's story about his past week.

Doctor sees reality of poor daily

"Doctor Sees Reality of Poor" article

Dr. Rita Rodgers was genuinely concerned about the plight of the poor, just as her ancestors. Her grandfather, Dr. Gordon A. Rodgers, Sr., treated ailing patients who appeared on his front porch whom he knew couldn't pay. Her father, Dr. Samuel Rodgers, had served the poor every day of his professional career and was considered a health care reformist. "She's a Rodgers" was the sentiment echoed throughout her life.

The article read, "Dr. Rita Rodgers spent another Tuesday listening, nodding and tending to the ailment of patients many other physicians would rather not touch." The article described a typical male patient "without a dime's worth of insurance" who arrives at the appointment with a high blood pressure reading, a worn red bag that held his medicine, and a sandwich. Reality means indigent patients who must choose between food, rent, shoes for the kids and medicine for themselves.

The patient offered, "You can stretch the medication out if you need to," his voice slurred by a stroke a few years ago. Rodgers scribbled a prescription and shook her head. "That's not a good idea. But that's reality," she said.

The article outlined the treatment costs and sources of payment for patients. Currently only 2 percent of US physicians worked in the public sector. This is not the type of practice you aspire to in medical school, she explained. "Nobody really talks about working in the inner city or in rural areas." Private physicians and hospitals were increasingly resisting the bureaucratic hassles of treating Medicaid and Medicare patients. These conditions represented the "quiet before the storm." Charles Schade of the American Public Health Association said in the article, "Just watch, public health physicians are going to be very, very busy."

Dr. Rita's clinic desk "doubles as a sink, barely large enough for a telephone, stapler, and morning mail. Stacks of medical records are heaped on an examination table." But she is much happier now than when she worked in a Houston HMO with mostly entitled middle-class patients. Her better instincts brought her back home to Kansas City to work at the clinic headed by her father, Dr. Sam Rodgers. A man in the "right place at the right time" on the leading edge of the next horizon in public health, and now he was not alone.

CAN WE JUST TALK

"A lot of what my patients need is someone they can talk to," Rita said. "A health problem is just another blow in their lives, one more tragedy to deal with."

As I read my sister's words, I was struck by similar conversations with my father decades ago. "There is often not a medical diagnosis; they just simply needed to talk," my father would say.

Father and daughter would soon join forces in administrative roles at SURHC, the dream Sam and his father shared that was not allowed to manifest. Who could stop it now?

"A dream may be held at the focal point of one's thinking and planning, until at last a man becomes the living embodiment of what he dreams. This is the first miracle: a man becomes his dream."

HOWARD THURMAN

THE SUNSET
(1996–1999)

The Journey at Sunset

When is the journey for accessible health and human rights over? Does it begin and end with the loss of its founder, or does it reappear anew everyday like the sun, still lighting the way? It was indeed the North Star that continued to provide continuous connections on my father's journey northward as he followed his true calling he never lost sight of. The temporary journey on earth ended for my father, but the strength and purpose of his vision lives on.

"Men who have become embodiments of a dream project an institution that becomes the embodiment of that dream. It is of the very nature of such a dream that it continues to grow, to develop, to find ever more creative dimensions. Hence, the dream is always receding; it cannot be contained in one life, however perfect. (Howard Thurman, Meditations of the Heart, pg.42)

HOWARD THURMAN

DREAMS DO COME TRUE

SUR's dream to acquire specialty training to become a surgeon, his admittance on staff of a once-segregated hospital, and now his ultimate dream to transform a community with health care as the anchor—all became reality. He delivered babies for the same family's over multiple generations in Kansas City's black community, which, based on the current statistics for infant mortality, created a cornerstone of wellness from the start in their young lives.

SUR transferred his childhood "scuffles" from the streets of Anniston, Alabama, to the streets of Kansas City, Missouri, to fight for access to health care for people who did not have a voice. He desired to make a difference, wanting to do something at a much higher level to affect health care in Kansas City, and when he did, everyone benefited; that's what a leader with character and integrity can do.

In doing so he would draw people to champion his cause and was acknowledged by US presidents, senators, mayors, and public health associations who would recognize his efforts. In the years following his departure from the health center, the acknowledgments kept coming and continue until this day. Even so, my father remained his humble self, regarding these accolades as recognition of something he was humanely bound and expected to do for others. He saw access to health care as a human right for all; he was just the facilitator. My father lived from within, based on the deeply ingrained values he witnessed and learned as a child. Without the efforts of admiring colleagues and employees who renamed streets, awards, and buildings in his name, he would have been satisfied in knowing that one more person received the best medical care possible, delivered with respect.

MIRACLES HAPPEN

ACKNOWLEDGED BY PRESIDENTS, MAYORS, SENATORS

After SUR's well-documented efforts to dismantle the segregated battle grounds of Hospital Hill, he met and heard the words of President Harry S. Truman at the dedication of the Queen of the World Facilities at 3210 East 23rd Street, operated by the Maryknoll nuns. Archbishop O'Hara was praised by Mr. Truman for his leadership in bringing the dream of a non-segregated hospital to reality.

Dedication of Queen of the World Facilities

"This is something I looked forward to since I set my Congress on the civil rights bill, and even longer. There ought to be no lines drawn on the medical staffs and no lines drawn where human beings' lives are at stake. I shall fight for that as long as I live," said Truman. (The Kansas City Times, "NO MEDICAL BAR," Monday, May 23, 1955)

Mr. Truman said he hoped the example of the new hospital would be like a rock that has been thrown into a lake, causing ripples of understanding between races that will spread to every other city in the country.

SUR had fled Anniston in 1944 due to discrimination and lack of training opportunity. In 1955, he would stand with Harry S. Truman as a board-certified OB-GYN in a non-segregated hospital as the secretary-treasurer of Queen of the World Hospital.

EXECUTIVE DIRECTOR EMERITUS, NEWS ANNOUNCEMENTS

In 1996, after a thirty-plus year career providing health care in Kansas City, Dr. Samuel U. Rodgers stepped down as executive director of the health center, assuming the title of executive director emeritus. My sister, Rita Rodgers-Stanley, became the interim executive director. This news spread like wildfire, as announced in multiple news publications, each providing a different aspect of his life and career. It was a major news interest story in the health care world and among Kansas Citians in general, many of whom had been patients.

A December 1996 article entitled "Heaven Sent: Local Heroes Glorify Kansas City" (Ingram's Magazine, December

1996, pg. 35) argued that apart from the usual articles of leadership corruption and greed, there was instead a host of heroes who gave themselves and worked to lift Kansas City's spirits. Dr. Rodgers was one of eleven Kansas Citian's honored.

As the son of an Anniston, Alabama doctor, young SUR witnessed the needs of the poor, and what he saw would affect his work throughout his life.

Rodgers described hearing knocks on the door in the middle of the night and pleads. "Please come see my old lady. My wife's sick, Doc," the patient would say. "Sometimes they'd walk miles to the house. That's all I knew, and I understood that someone needed to take care of them. Poor people do not have a chance. If you're not going to help them, who the hell is?"

In 1967, Rodgers earned a master's degree in public health, returned to Kansas City, and opened the SURHC (then named Wayne Miner), a move described as an "anomaly" in the medical world. As noted in the article, "Today, few would argue about its success." The health center that opened in 1968, under the executive director leadership of Rodgers, now includes five sites located on Kansas City's east side and an enrollment of fifty thousand indigent or uninsured patients.

In his new advisory role as executive director emeritus, Rodgers worked with Truman Medical Center and the University of Missouri Kansas City School of Medicine and continued as an advocate for the poor.

I don't ever recall a time when my father stood still in one place without a mission in mind to pursue. He was strategic, with continuous projects in the pipeline—one always replacing the last. Even semi-retiring from the health center, he was involved in efforts to work with youth in addition to brokering new agreements that would broaden service opportunities for patients. SUR seemed to have a continuum of work but never looked stressed or overwhelmed.

FOLLOWING FATHER'S FOOTSTEPS

As Samuel U. Rodgers steps down as executive director of the community health center, his daughter, Rita Rodgers-Stanley, will temporarily fill the role. She is an internist who has worked at the center for seven years.

KEVIN ANDERSON/The Star

The article read, "FOLLOWING FATHER'S FOOT-STEPS." Though stepping down from the executive director position, my father made it clear that this was not a time for sadness. Rita explained, "He's still going to be working full time, but he gets a chance to do something he's always wanted to do: work with the young." (The Kansas City Star_ Section B-April 5, 1996, Melissa Bedford).

As Dr. Rodgers' announcement marked the end of twenty-nine years of leadership, the board of directors also approved a provider contract with Children's Mercy Hospital/Truman Medical Center Family Health Partners (HMO), an unusual action because provider contracts were typically agreements between "clinics" and HMOs. The health center brokered a broader agreement with Truman covering more than clinical services for patients. This new agreement would allow medical residents and medical students to undergo hands on training at the health center.

The agreement represented an unfathomable opportunity my father and colleagues could never have imagined in their clinical days. After twenty-nine years my father was still opening doors for others and making history in the process.

Eight months after my father stepped down, Dr. Rita, interim executive director of SURHC, was named permanently to the post after an exhaustive national search. The board of directors of SURHC voted unanimously to select Dr. Rita as the center's executive director. (The Call Newspaper—December 1996—Vol. 77, No. 20)

Dr. Jay Backstrom, MD, MPH, chairman of the board of directors, explained that a five-member search committee attracted qualified candidates from across the US, narrowing the field to three outstanding finalists. "Rita was selected because she is the best qualified person for this position."

The article "Community Health Pioneers Retires" announced Dr. Rodgers, the seventy-nine-year-old obstetrician-gynecologist, was retiring after more than a half century of service to the people of Kansas City. Dr. Samuel U. Rodgers developed the federally assisted community health center. (NACHCLINK—Winter 1997 Vol. 3, No. 4-James W. Couch)

Dr. Rodgers was described as "one of the handful of reform-minded physicians" who understood that a new model of health care was needed to fight poverty and ensure quality medical care became accessible to everyone. Per the National Association of Community Health Centers (NACHC) article, "He embraced the community-based health center model as a way to join resources of governments and communities to bring doctors and basic health services into areas of greatest need—America's inner cities, migrant farmworker communities, and rural isolated areas."

In 1978, NACHC honored our father with a special award established in his name, the Samuel U. Rodgers Achievement Award for Dedication and Excellence in the Field of Community Health Care Delivery.

The Serendipity Photo

THE SERENDIPITY PHOTO

Included in the NACHC article was a keepsake photograph entitled "Dr. Samuel U. Rodgers, Executive Director Emeritus and Rita Rodgers-Stanley, MD, Interim Executive Director of SURHC, Kansas City, MO greet President Bill Clinton on his recent visit to the city." This memorable picture would appear in multiple news publications and became even more special February 10, 2021, when Dr. Rita shared a social media story, written and posted by the photographer who captured this historic moment. It was indeed a moment of serendipity that created an opportunity.

Serendipitous moments of grace through storytelling of my family history took center court in my writings. As I would soon acknowledge, the back story *is* the story. My surprise was as I wrote, additional stories would surface and find their way to me, presenting an embarrassment of riches in information. As I wrote about my father's life as I knew it, this story continued to grow and write itself. My father positively touched more lives than he knew, and they all had stories to share, which continues today. It didn't matter how or in what capacity my father would meet someone; he offered the same level of respectability to all, a learned family value. One such story was that of professional photographer Debbie Douglass Sauer whose social media post was forwarded to my attention by my sister. Should we ever meet, I want Ms. Sauer to know I will never look at this photo the same way again. Debbie Sauers' post entitled "The Story Behind Photo!" captured the backstory of that day.

As described by Sauer in her Facebook post, "I've photographed many Presidents, but this story is about Dr. Samuel U. Rodgers and what a great man he was! Over the years I photographed Dr. Sam many times. This particular time was when President Clinton was going to be in Kansas City to speak about health care in our country to a large group at the Ritz."

President Clinton visited Kansas City to speak about health care to a large group, followed by a smaller group of health care experts, which included Dr. Sam and Dr. Rita. Ms. Sauer, asked by her PR client to get a photo of Clinton and the Rodgers, had not asked for press credentials, nor did she have a big camera that day.

"Instead, I just had a point and shoot camera in my pocket and went in with Dr. Sam and Dr. Rita in a side door that led into another side door by a Secret Service person that we happened to know!" Debbie said.

The group was led into a small room of ten circled chairs, then between a set of blue curtains that opened into an even smaller five-foot-wide area. While the group stood waiting, a different Secret Service person arrived notably agitated about their presence, informing Debbie, "You can't be here." The SS person finally agreed but limited her to one photo. She countered, proposing two.

Suddenly, a man with ten cameras around his neck entered the small, curtained space. A few seconds later President Clinton's hand parted the curtains where Debbie stood, and she quickly introduced the group and their purpose. Debbie immediately snapped two photos, and per Murphy's law, someone blinked in one of the two photos, and the plan B mission was accomplished. Moreover, Debbie Douglas Sauer would add to my treasure trove of memories.

My father was extremely happy that the health center was able to attract and keep a physician with Rita's experience in the community health center movement. He knew his daughter's commitment to the mission and to public health in general made her an excellent choice for executive director of the health center.

My sister was indeed an excellent choice for more reasons than one. Not only did she have the medical credentials and diverse work experience, but she also had family values you couldn't buy or sell. She is—like my father—compassionate and genuinely, palpably caring to the core. My mind flashed back to a childhood scene where four-year-old Rita, arms wrapped around the sad loser, would console a teary-eyed playmate who had lost at a game. "Don't cry. It's okay," she would say in a reassuring tone, the same supportive tone she uses with her trusting patients today. She was a natural humanitarian from the start, no coaching needed.

The Setting Sun

The daily disappearance of the sun, known as sunset, shows us both the passage of time and represents the completion of a day's work. The deep colors of the sky at sunset are symbolic of the beauty and the mystery of life itself. No two sunsets look alike, each beautiful in the colors it brings. Sunset is temporary and often taken for granted because it happens every day. There is no mystery in death as we know it is imminent. So why are we never prepared?

SUR'S ILLNESS, PATIENT CARE

Shortly after my mother's death, around 1985, my father was diagnosed with prostate cancer believed to be manageable if treated early. Our family learned many lessons through the example of my mother's illness, and second and third opinions were sought. After weighing all options, Dr. Rodgers sought treatment at MD Anderson Cancer Center (MDACC) in Houston Texas, still ranked number one in 2022. Rita's 2.5-year residency at University of Texas Health Science Center had included several rotations through MD Anderson. We visited her at MDACC during the early stages of my mother's cancer diagnosis, while she could still travel.

My mother proudly witnessed Rita in action as a resident—white coat and all—during a family trip to Houston, one of her last.

The Houston treatment plan "countered" the original KC diagnosis treatment plan for SUR, and he began treatment in Houston. The bi-annual checkups continued for several years. He found joy and satisfaction in these visits as they presented an opportunity to witness patient care in another setting and take note of the patient-friendly approaches implemented at MD Anderson. He was now the patient, a health center executive, and a perpetual student.

With each visit my father would be warmly greeted by the medical staff—now like family—who would marvel at his state of health. He would chuckle while imitating their greeting, "Dr. Rodgers, you're back again. How are you feeling?" they said with amazement in their voices at his continued progress.

"Doing great. Did you think I'd be gone by now?" my father would reply. My father was later awarded the Patient Navigation Award.

He returned home grateful for his Houston patient experiences, giving credit where credit was due. He explained that upon exiting his car he was visually guided via parking lot graphics, from his origin to the desired clinic destination. Non-ambulatory patients were met immediately by medical staff who would put them at immediate ease. These are the patient care efficiencies my father marveled at—that put a smile of satisfaction on his face, just knowing patients were being respectfully cared for.

THE BEST-MADE PLANS

In 1998, my brother and I—Atlanta residents—looked forward to a white Christmas in Kansas City as we did every year. Our careers and educational endeavors brought us south, but Kansas City was still home, even with our mother's passing in 1985. We looked forward to experiencing the Christmas tree lighting at the Country Club Plaza, visiting Topsy's Popcorn, and of course, Gates & Sons BBQ. Gates was a family tradition, and we would make a stop there as we left the airport prior to proceeding to our 3405 Quincy home.

Days before our Atlanta departure, the unimaginable happened. I received a call that my brother had been taken to the emergency room. These occasional ER visits were not unusual, and I thought it perfect timing given our upcoming flight in two days. IV hydration always provided an immunity boost to my brother's bouts with chronic pneumonia. I didn't rush to the hospital having experienced these routine visits before. Instead, I took the time to pack a bag of snacks and a book, as the hospital was a mere ten-minute drive from my home. My arrival at the emergency room was preceded by a first cousin who reported Rickey was displaying his usual feistiness complaining of the thin blankets.

I laughed and said, "What else is new? That's great! He must be feeling much better," I said with a sigh of relief. I had hoped this was a sign that this particular emergency room visit would be a short one, leaving the rest of the afternoon for packing.

When it was my turn to visit the ER, what I encountered was not at all what I expected. A doctor entered quickly, dismissively asking, "You do understand what's going on?" with no further explanation, before quickly departing the ER. I would never see him again.

Puzzled, I returned to my brother's bedside, sitting, and holding his hand. As we locked our eyes on each other, he mouthed inaudible words, his lungs filled with fluid. His big, trademark expressive eyes were fixed on mine, and suddenly, he was gone. Around 11 o'clock, within fifteen minutes of my ER arrival, my big brother, my guardian angel and "always protector," was no more.

I wanted to scream but instead just sobbed alone in the exam room at the inevitability of life. I believe he waited for me before passing. I made my way across the room to the wall phone and called Rita. Who could feel what I was feeling but my sister? We were after all the Three R's. It was the longest wait I would ever know.

"Hello...hello?" she said. For what seemed like an eternity I closed my eyes and could finally whisper, "Rickey's gone... please let Daddy know." It was a short visit after all.

The Three R's photographed at home, Rickey

The Three R's photographed at home

I imagined my brother chasing me playfully throughout our house, at ages ten and seven. I was the "scream" at the receiving end of my brother's pranks, which made it all worth his while. I was the one he threw into the deep end of the pool, where I quickly learned to tread water in that moment, because he believed I could. He would stand at pool side, poised for a rescue maneuver in case his predictions failed him. Rickey rescued me and my car in the frigid cold winters from the bottom of Quincy Street, as my car tires stuck in the icy snow. The steepness of Quincy—a hill few could conquer in the snow—never proved a challenge to him.

I don't know how I drove back home the morning he died. I was behind the wheel for sure, but my hope of that carefree morning drive had turned to feelings of despair by noon. The world looked oddly different now, and I knew it would never be the same again. Big parts of my childhood memories had departed with Rickey. Who could understand? On December 21, 1998, the Delta flight took off as planned to carry my brother's body. I sat alone on the plane.

The Parting

SUR'S DEATH

The Samuel U. Rodgers Community Health Center and the entire Kansas City community suffered a great loss in the passing of its founder, Samuel U. Rodgers, MD, MPH, on December 19, 1999. As the sunset represents the completion of a day, my father's death represented the completion of his human life but not of his vision that lives on daily as witnessed through the administration efforts at the health center he founded that continues to prosper. My father's life had provided such an example and hope; now what would be the impact of his death?

SURHC Building at sunset

In December 2021, while at home in Atlanta, I revisited my file drawer of memories again and again as I continued to write, pulling various subject matter as needed, discovering each time an overlooked article. On a peaceful Sunday afternoon, I accessed the same files, this time to find a bright pink church program. I had no memory of having saved this program and couldn't figure out why I did. In one glance at the church program the memories of this most unique church experience instantly returned.

THE ST. JAMES IMPARTATION

In 1999, I had big hopes and plans for a joyous and restful Christmas season; nothing, I hoped, like the Christmas of 1998. My husband was employed in Chicago, and I in Atlanta; we enjoyed a commuter marriage. We planned to spend several days in Chicago after my arrival, prior to flying to KC to spend the Christmas holidays with my family. We planned to leave the following Monday. My husband, an Episcopalian, suggested we attend Sunday church service at a neighborhood church in downtown Chicago.

On that extremely cold, windy but sunny Chicago morning, we were more than relieved to enter through the doors of St. James Episcopal Church, 65 E. Huron Street. Having never attended this church, I was transfixed on the beauty of it the moment I entered. Its ordinary exterior did not prepare me for what I would see and experience inside. I took several steps inside and couldn't resist looking upward to the golden-arched trusses and the yellow-and-green-glazed ceramic brick that covered the walls. It was a simple yet breathtaking cathedral without being ostentatious. The sun shone across the church doing justice to the warm pastel colors, deepened by the bright sunlight. The church smelled of incense and candles and felt comfortable, warm, and welcoming. I took a seat near the end of the pew, in the mid-section of the church, enjoying the peaceful surroundings on the fourth Sunday of Advent. The painted patterns of the church walls and ceiling were reminiscent of a brocade fabric that had been stenciled with a sponge. I felt wrapped in a beautiful fabric, and then the prayer "Magnificat" was read, followed by the processional hymn, "Veni, Emmanuel" ("O Come, O Come, Emmanuel").

I was lost in the reverie of the music and memories of my brother's Morehouse Glee Club performances. I remembered the many MGC concerts sponsored by the Samuel U. Rodgers Health Center at the Folly Theater. I prayed I could turn back the hands of time thinking only of my brother and his love of music. I closed my eyes, absorbed in the sounds, to be suddenly disturbed by a sunbeam that landed across my face. I squirmed to move out of the line of light to no avail as the pew was full. At that moment I heard the words that appeared to be audible only to me.

"Your brother is coming to get your father. Don't worry; everything is going to be alright."

Kappa Boule Party—SUR and the Three R's

The service ended, and the message about my brother was forgotten before I exited the church. I dismissed it all as a fleeting thought, a daydream. My husband and I returned home following church, to hear a worrying message on the voice recording from my sister.

The voice recording message played, "Daddy has not been the same today; he did not arise as usual and is not interested in eating. I've called the nurse and don't know what to do."

After phoning my sister, I immediately booked a flight to KC that afternoon and hurried to O'Hare Airport. As I nervously waited at the boarding gate, I received the call.

"Daddy's gone," Rita said.

In that moment, I released a sound that was unrecognizable even to me—not caring who heard or watched.

THE DIVINING REVELATION

I arrived in KC in blizzard conditions and traveled safely to my sister and brother-in-law's home, just a few miles from Kansas City International (KCI). SUR had been under their care for over two weeks at their rural North Kansas City home. Rita had located a hospital bed in a space at the rear of her house, where my father could look across the expansive three-acre backyard.

When I arrived at the KCI gate, I automatically searched for my father as I had done for years, to be abruptly reminded that he had passed away just hours earlier. My father would stop whatever he was doing to meet us at the Kansas City International Airport each visit, now a family tradition. "Oh Daddy, you don't need to drive me to the airport." "Someone else can take me, don't worry." He would have it no other way. With each visit he waited at the gate, straining to see me as I deboarded the plane, and I him. Now when I land at KCI, I pretend I can still see him standing there, waiting, and watching. Although I know he's not there, I still smile and wave in the direction of the concourse where he used to wait for me. He represented my gateway home, my welcome home committee of one, being the first and last, I would see. He was my "face of Kansas City."

After my father relocated to Rita's home, he would ask peri-odically, "Now, all I need to do is look out the window and enjoy and watch the birds."

"Yes, Daddy that's all," we would respond with a smile.

For once in his life, he had time to be a focused bird watcher. Still, he asked daily, "How's the health center?"

My father had always cared for the birds and every morn-ing would make sure his backyard bird feeder was packed full of seed and suet during the winter, before heading to the hospital.

Upon my arrival on Robinhood Lane, I was relieved to see Rita, now the only one who could truly understand the new void in my heart at my father's passing.

"I was torn about whether to call you at the airport with the news," she said.

Our father's body remained at Rita's home for hours after his death due to inclement weather and impassable roadways. Rita and I sat together, holding hands at my father's bedside, resigned to our new reality, as we recounted the activities of the day.

"I am so glad you were with him." I sat back and listened, exhausted by this single day that felt like three days in one, but it was still Sunday, December 19, 1999. "He never got out of bed, nor did he eat. His eyes opened as he looked toward the window, focusing intently on something as if watching a movie screen, and he passed away hours later," my sister said.

We sat in silence until I said, "What time was that?"

"Around 11:00," Rita would remember.

Slowly pondering Rita's words, I was finally able to connect my Chicago church experience that morning to her morning recollections. I shared the message with Rita I had received in church around 11 o'clock. It was only at this moment that I could fully appreciate the message meant only for me.

We looked wide-eyed at each other, taking a deep breath of resignation, trying to comprehend what happened in that special moment.

"Of course…who else would come?" we virtually said in unison.

Richard Rodgers, APD Police

Rickey, the Missouri state patrolman and motorcycle-riding Atlanta Police Department (APD) officer, would be the one to escort our father into the light. Rickey was our protector and now our family's guardian angel. We could rest assured as Rickey would not have it any other way. In Rickey's earthly job responsibilities, he had escorted US presidents, vice presidents, and mayors in his APD motorcycle brigade.

DAUGHTERS

We remained at our father's bedside, remembering who he was as a person. We knew he was much more than the remarkable doctor who had cared for so many. We walked down memory lane from my father's childhood home at 1618 Cooper Avenue in Anniston, Alabama, to our childhood home at 3405 Quincy. Our father was an intentional man who led and taught by example. He set his daughters up for success without our realization in the moment. He wanted true success for us, not only materialistic gain. He desired we become our own persons, believing we would achieve whatever we set our minds to while remaining concerned about the wellbeing of others, just as he had. I would like to believe Rita and I have become the women we all envisioned.

Education was foremost, and at the ages of eleven and twelve, we found ourselves enrolled at Loretto Academy (LA). LA was a Montessori-based all-girls school run by the sisters of Loretto at the Foot of the Cross. We were excited about attending Loretto, as we had other friends attending as well and thought that was reason enough. My father's bigger vision was to provide his daughters with an unconventional education, one that would build their confidence as women and give them freedom of voice. SUR had been raised by an independent woman, his mother Fannie Mamie. His philosophy was that women have a unique voice that should be expressed in this world—used to speak their mind, and stand up for themselves, as their lives mattered too.

We would boast and marvel at our opportunity to work at the McDonalds in the inner city, where life lessons of people's struggles abounded, in disbelief that our parents had ever allowed this. While conducting interviews in 2021 for this book, I learned my father had hired Everitt O'Neal as security detail at the health center. To our surprise Mr. Everitt O'Neal's security office was located across the street from McDonalds, in easy sight of our employment. My father let us experience life to learn the much-needed lessons, while always finding a way to ensure our safety. We thought all these choices were ours.

MIDNIGHT PARTING

It was a little after midnight when the funeral hearse arrived. It was only befitting that Bruce Watkins, Jr. safely arrived on Robinhood Lane to transport our father's body to the Watkins funeral home. "Brucie," as we had called him since childhood, a lifelong friend, hugged us as he entered. The three of us looked at each other knowingly; it was finally time to say goodbye. Following Bruce's departure, Rita and I continued to share memories well into the wee morning hours—now December 20, 1999.

Three R's on horseback, Watkins Family Ranch

Suddenly December 19, 1998, memories forcefully returned. Turning in disbelief to face Rita, I whispered, "Daddy died on the same day as Rickey; exactly one year apart around the same morning hour between ten and eleven o'clock a.m. on December 19; Rickey in 1998, Daddy in 1999…a date and day we will never forget."

We hugged each other tightly and prepared ourselves for another Christmas season of mourning and celebration of the lives they both led. Puzzled, I turned toward Rita and said, "I don't pretend to understand these happenings; but I am responsible for sharing this story, because it happened."

"God will allow certain things to happen… Whatever he can do to bring comfort to those moments he will do through ministering spirits assigned to us—angels who are there for our comfort and protection," Rita responded.

Rita's wisdom was enough revelation for me.

Celebration of Life

SUR's standing-room-only funeral was held on December 27, 1999, at the Watkins Brothers Memorial Chapel with Pastor Sam Mann officiating. Watkins, the same chapel where we celebrated my mother's life fourteen years before, was owned and operated by Mr. and Mrs. Bruce and Jewel Watkins, who were long time family friends. A caravan of our Anniston family arrived in full force, bringing comfort and love as they had for a lifetime, as did the Pullams, my mother's side of the family. I delivered a heartfelt tribute to my father, at least what was left of my heart that day. It helped to speak my thoughts out loud into the universe, as if releasing my words might alter my new reality of life without him for the first time. What might speaking out loud accomplish?

The honorary pallbearers included my father's faithful friends and colleagues, Drs. W.R. and Carl Peterson, Starks Williams, W. Filmore Haith, all of whom eventually came to work for my father at SURHC. Jim Nunnelly, my father's devoted mentee from his early twenties, was the only non-family member invited to serve as an active pallbearer.

Dr. Samuel Ulysses Rodgers

Memorial Services Held At
WATKINS BROTHERS MEMORIAL
CHAPEL
Monday, December 27, 1999
2:00 PM

Pastor Sam Mann
Officiating

Funeral Program—Watkins Funeral Home

It was a quiet and solemn event. Reverend Samuel Mann, born and raised in Alabama, delivered the eulogy. Rev. Mann had spent years in KC as a pastor and advocate for social justice. He and my father, the two "Sams" from small-town Alabama, had both made a difference in this inner-city community. Rev. Mann, a civil rights activist and eloquent spiritual leader, chaired the Southern Christian Leadership Conference on race relations and marched with MLK.

Rev. Mann spoke of my father's works, describing his disciple-like qualities. Rev. Mann, a white pastor, had ministered to a predominately black congregation at St. Mark Union Church located just blocks from the health center. Rev. Mann had watched the construction of the health center, built brick by brick. Mann knew the struggles of the surrounding community firsthand through the pastoring of the families that resided there. He also witnessed life changing family moments, as health care was made accessible at one's doorstep through SURHC.

Rita and I believed the two Sam's to be kindred spirits and could not think of a better person to eulogize SUR. My father, a doctor and civil rights activist, used health care as the cornerstone for community transformation. Rev. Mann, a civil rights activist, used the principles of Christianity as tools of transformation. My father would also utilize the principles of Christianity in a non-conventional way outside the walls of the church by living his religion out loud for everyone to see and benefit from. During his eulogy of SUR, Rev. Mann referred to him as one of God's apostles, one who walked among the poor doing God's work. As Rev. Mann spoke, I smiled inside as I could imagine my father finding humor in this saintly comparison.

Our family was again blessed by the presence and friendship of Oleta Adams. I traveled back in time to see my entire family seated at the Crown Center Hotel enjoying a memorable evening with Oleta, mesmerized by her voice that pulled at the deepest recesses of your heart. On this special day her comforting voice would again penetrate my spirit as she sang, "Everything Must Change" and "To Dream the Impossible Dream" in tribute to SUR. My father had dreamed of becoming what was a seemingly impossible dream of wanting to become a surgeon when there seemingly was no way forward. SUR had dreamed of making health care accessible to people of color and an ignored immigrant population;

and through this vision he did, Jim would say. The program closing read:

Blessed are the pure in heart, for they shall see God. Blessed are the peacemakers, for they shall be called sons of God.

MATTHEW 5: 8–9

INTERMENT: FOREST HILL CEMETERY

On the processional drive to the cemetery, I stared blankly out of the window at the bleakness of the day, with below-zero temperatures. To distract myself, I reached for my purse-sized Bible and opened it to Matthew 2:16, the befitting bookmarked funeral scripture, that reads:

"As Jesus reclined at the table, many tax collectors and sinners came and dined with Jesus and the disciples. When the scribes of the Pharisees saw this, they asked, 'Why is he eating and drinking with tax collectors and sinners' Hearing this, Jesus said to them, 'It is not those who are healthy that need a physician, but those who are sick....'"

My father stood his ground for his rights and the rights of poor communities of color regarding health care because it was the right and decent thing to do. He dined with "tax collectors and sinners," eventually changing the hearts and minds of many previously indifferent or willfully ignorant to the plight of the poor. Everyone had a right to receive health care.

The entourage of cars proceeded to the Forest Hill Cemetery graveside service. Shortly after our arrival, we were informed that due to the inclement temperatures there could be no burial in the frozen soil. I lost my last opportunity to say an official goodbye to Daddy, as I turned and walked away. The mourners returned to their cars and the limousine entourage slowly proceeded toward the exit. Emotionally exhausted from the previous days, I closed my eyes, resting my head against the back of the seat.

Unexpectedly, the exiting stream of limousine cars came to a stop. Curious, I peered out of the window noticing that my car had stopped in view of a small elaborate stone structure.

Believing that I could see what appeared to be my father's casket, I yelled, "Wait, wait," and opened the car door and bolted from the limousine.

I ran carefully along the icy driveway leading to the covered area and entered through the arched opening. Stunned and breathless, I stood at the foot of my father's casket alone. Because there could be no burial that day in frozen soil, my father's casket rested here giving me another chance to say goodbye. The wind chill factor was five degrees below zero, and I watched my breath condense in the air, as I felt my tears—burning as they ran down my cheeks.

"Goodbye and thank you for giving me life," I finally said as I departed.

I knew his spirit had passed on, yet I didn't want him to be left all alone in this cold place. I rested my gloved hand on the casket and prayed, thanking God for the life of this most incredible man. My cries, weakened after days of mourning, were magnified against the frozen walls of the stone enclosure. I had escaped my grief for only a short moment, knowing life would never be the same again. I didn't want to let go, nor could I imagine a life without my father. Rita and I, now alone as the remaining members of our immediate family, still had each other to weave together the memories of the lives that had gone before us.

SUR was undoubtedly special to us as our father, but he was also a rare and unique bird among men. An exotic species and blend of personal character and values that I might never be as close to again. He was a prince among men. Moreover, I was holding on to the ideals of compassion, decency, and goodness all in one person. Would we ever see these characteristics embodied in a single person who loved us as much as he did?

As I chronicled the miraculous happenings of December 19, 1999, I couldn't overlook the abundance of "nines" and became curious about the meaning of this number. What I learned put a smile on my face and a knowing joy in my heart. The field of numerology associates the spiritual meaning of nine as a sign of commitment in service to humanity using your natural ability as you look for ways to help others in a positive way. The energy of nine represented completion, not finality. I thought about the continued success and future of the health center after our father's death, achieving milestone goals annually with many new plans on the horizon. Life was not over by any account.

Remembrance

WHO WAS SUR?

I no longer wonder "why" my father was bound and determined to accomplish what he did, nor "how" he accomplished his vision to make health care affordable and accessible to underserved patient populations. It was both his personal calling and mission, matched with an experiential and educational preparedness that positioned him in the right place at the right time, creating a man with a vision. Dr. Rodgers' impact on the greater Kansas City and national public health communities, health center employees, and medical colleagues was unquestionable.

The influence felt was indeed multifaceted, varying by individual and circumstance. However, the lifetime impact of his presence became an indelible footprint in the hearts and memories, of the people who knew and worked with him, as they would share decades later in their own words. What is truly received in another person's spirit has been transferred through genuine care given from the heart. My father's caring heart transformed and influenced many lives and circumstances because they felt his care.

Nina Ballew Howard was uniquely suited for this interview that my sister and I conducted virtually on February 4, 2021. She'd had a full-circle experience of everything SURHC had to offer from multiple perspectives. Her health center journey began as a young newcomer to Kansas City, Missouri.

NINA BALLEW HOWARD: LOUISVILLE, KENTUCKY

I first met Nina Ballew in 1981 at an inner-city McDonald's hamburger franchise. Rita, Nina, and I were all fifteen to sixteen years old when we began working at McDonald's hamburgers. I had no way of knowing that Nina—or Rita— would eventually make a career at the health center. Nina, originally from Louisville, Kentucky, and her family had recently relocated to KC for her stepfather's new job. While driving through town one Saturday they would hear a KPRS radio broadcast announcing the Cancer-Rama Health Fair

(CHF) event. CHF was administered jointly by Dr. Rodgers, Jim Nunnelly, and Rev. James Tindall from the Jackson County Legislature (JCL). Nina's family attended the health fair that same day. As shared forty years later during our interview, "That's when I first met Dr. Rodgers; I was fifteen years old."

In 1993, Nina became the full-time health fair coordinator of the CHF event. "That's how I got to Wayne Miner Health Center (WMHC)." Nina assisted Clara Maddox, who was very experienced with the inner workings of the health fair, until Clara retired in 1994. Nina explained the health fair began with twenty-five participating vendors and grew to 250. A three-mile "family fun walk" was eventually added to the fair led by Sam Rodgers, through the streets of the community. Later a "Kidsville" event was sponsored at the nearby Woodland Elementary School, in addition to a KPRS radio talent showcase and the participation of local churches and choirs.

"Dr. Rodgers was a part of every bit of it—from the very beginning," Nina said with pride. Channel 4, the local news station, became one of the fair's biggest sponsors, providing a live one-hour telecast. The health care event grew in attendance to five thousand people. There was an activity for everyone regardless of age in the surrounding community, and more importantly, there was access to exams and medical testing at no charge. "Many people of color never saw a doctor until they were sick, so the fair was an effort to establish a health baseline," Nina added. The patients could then be referred to a doctor for treatment or become patients at SURHC.

In 1991 and 1992, then-Jackson County legislator James Tindall placed Nina Howard at Rodgers for six months each year to organize the city-wide health fair. In 1993, Nina was placed at Rodgers permanently, where she was responsible for the creation and administration of innovative outreach activities. In 2000, Nina was named "Director of Community Access and Engagement" and retired on December 31, 2020, after over twenty-six years of dedicated service.

Nina was the impetus behind the creation of the Samuel U. Rodgers Legacy Award, awarded to civic-minded individuals who were community focused. In 2018, Nina was also the force behind the street renaming on Euclid Avenue, now called Honorary Samuel U. Rodgers Ave. "The change required signatures from surrounding organizations, but it was so simple because everyone in the neighborhood loved your Daddy," she explained.

Nina recalled her favorite film, a reel-to-reel video created by Dr. Rodgers entitled "Marsha," a wonderful tool used to train new hires. "Marsha" was a black lady who lived in the projects and took long bus rides to the hospital due to lack of transportation. The film showed Marsha sitting all day at the hospital to be seen by a doctor, only to take long bus rides back home to the projects. "This was why Dr. Rodgers wanted the clinic—so people could receive medical care in their community." For this reason, Nina considered the SURHC, a "health center in the community for the people." Nina knew of the importance of medical access in an underserved community firsthand, growing up in Kentucky.

"We lived in the country, and as a child I remember my mother bartering with cabbage from the garden for a doctor's house call. My mom became a patient at the WMHC starting with our KC arrival in 1981 until her death in 2007, a twenty-six-year patient of the center who lived across the street. She went to Rodgers because she felt safe. She loved Dr. Rita who became her doctor. I trusted your daddy; I trusted what he said." Nina's brother and sister would eventually work at SURHC, where her grandchildren would also become patients.

SUR'S PERSONAL AND PROFESSIONAL IMPACT

Nina, a busy single parent admittedly without much training or background, was thrust into a situation she was uncertain she could handle. "Dr. Rodgers didn't talk a lot, but when he spoke, you knew it really meant something." Dr. Rodgers encouraged me, "Nina, never say can't; can't is not in your vocabulary. You can do anything you set your mind to." And she did.

Education, a lifetime priority for my father, was also an expectation of the workforce hired at SURHC, many of whom did not have a high school diploma. He desired an educated and self-sustaining community. "If they came to work, they also had to go to school. Your dad taught them how to fish," Nina explained.

My father wanted employees to benefit and gain something from this work experience, apart from a paycheck. Moreover, he valued education as freedom and sustenance; the one thing no one could ever take away.

Nina applauded the expansion of Rodgers' health care facilities to different geographical areas of Kansas City, while cautioning and hopeful the core community would not be forgotten. I don't feel like we're in our community any longer; we got lost someplace. Nina expressed hope that the center would return to some of the basics of earlier years. She offered a down-home analogy to make her point that I will not soon forget.

Nina acknowledged the time-saving convenience of making gravy using canned mushroom soup. However, often its more satisfying to return to the basics. "Every so often I like to put the flour inside the drippings and make gravy from scratch the old fashion way. Although it takes more time, it's the more worthwhile solution. Sometimes we need to go back to where we began to figure out how to move forward."

Dr. Rodgers' dream was to ensure that people—regardless of race creed or color—receive the health care they needed, where they were. We need to maintain his vision of "family first." Dr. Rodgers cared about people.

"SURHC is a great place, and your daddy's legacy will live on."

DR. DAVID SATCHER: INTERVIEW, DECEMBER 2, 2021

David Satcher grew up in Calhoun County, Alabama, a stone's throw away from Anniston, and knew members of the Rodgers family. Dr. Satcher was reminiscent of our father and grandfather in disposition, and a down-home example of decency, integrity, and purpose.

Dr. Satcher first recalled meeting SUR's father, Dr. Gordon A. Rodgers, Sr., during his application process for Morehouse College as a teenager. Satcher was informed by Morehouse that he would need to see a dentist as part of the admission process. Satcher described growing up on a forty-acre farm outside of Anniston, Alabama, raised by parents, neither of whom had attended elementary school. Morehouse had never had a student from a county or a training school. "Well, I finally got into Morehouse, but I wouldn't have if your grandfather hadn't signed the papers that he had examined my mouth and thought I would survive. Your grandfather, Dr. Gordon Rodgers, Sr., was great man. It was very inspirational to talk with him; I'll never forget that."

Several decades later, Satcher met Gordon A. Rodgers, Jr. at the Meharry Medical School's fiftieth year class reunion. During a Meharry alumni visit to Kansas City years later, he met Dr. Samuel U. Rodgers, who provided a personal tour of the Baseball Hall of Fame in the 18th and Vine historic district and the health center. "Your father was an amazing man, an inspiration to meet and talk to. His attitude toward health care was one that I appreciated."

"Dr. Samuel Rodgers thought people deserved quality health care and did everything he could to make sure that it happened. We are definitely kindred spirits. It was obvious he cared about people and acted on that caring. Your father is one of the best examples of somebody who made it clear from the beginning, that he cared about people who needed care whether they had money or not."

In closing I wanted Dr. Satcher to know Samuel and Gordon Rodgers regarded him as a son, had followed his successes and attended his surgeon general induction ceremony in Washington, DC. They were proud that another achieving son of the South really cared and exhibited the qualities of a person and leader with integrity.

In that moment I imagined hearing the song made famous by Mahalia Jackson, "If I Can Help Somebody."

Leadership, SUR Style

CHARACTERISTICS OF MY FATHER:

My father was many things to many people. He represented a force to be reckoned with among the established medical elite and power brokers at times. He was a straight shooter with no hidden agenda. An empathetic man with an unstoppable assignment whose time had come. Above all, he was trusted, credible, honest, caring, strategic, transparent, on mission, and boldly unapologetic about his cause. Professionally, these values translated into the making of a reform-minded physician, national authority, and outspoken advocate leader, as regarded by many colleagues. He was a calm and understated presence. Issues that raised his ire consistently involved the maltreatment of those who could not speak for themselves, people disregarded and ignored, or the powerful who could easily rectify the situation but chose to look the other way instead. Then and only then could you glimpse the fire within him that stoked his spirit, coming from the many generational rivers and streams of ancestors that made him who he was. He was a steadfast proponent of the poor and underserved.

Samuel Rodgers, M.D.
xecutive Director, Samuel U. Rodgers Health Center Inc.; Clinical Professor
bstetrics/Gynecology, University of Missouri-Kansas City School of Medicine
ounding Member and Executive Board Member, National Association of Commun
y Health Centers; Member, Missouri Coalition of Community and Migrant Health
enters; Honors: Wayne Miner Health Center officially renamed "Samuel U
odgers Health Center," 1988; Ambassador of Hope, Award of Courage, Americar

SUR Leadership Awards

These leadership attributes made him an influencer of people, professionally and personally. His interest was in the better-ment of the human condition, for people from all walks of life and cultures. He was fascinated by the study of human behavior and spent hours reading and sharing his thoughts with me in many conversations.

His real-life laboratory was witnessed in the many friend-ships and alliances he forged between people of unlikely beginnings for the goodwill of all. He wanted to know what made people tick, how individuals navigated their unique life's journey from beginning to end. Many visible needs existed that had to be addressed. He was not pretentious, boastful, or arrogant, nor blinded by the love of power, money, or material things. Naturally power, money and material things came his way, as grace would have it. These things manifested accordingly as proof of his character and integrity, but materialism never led the way.

Sail boating, SUR

He never looked down on anyone but into the eyes of everyone respectfully, knowing that each had something special to teach and contribute. He was never one to toot his own horn as he viewed his mission to provide health care to underserved communities as an unquestionable responsibility—who wouldn't? There were those who followed his vision and signed up for this mission (no questions asked), out of appreciation for what this health care giant slayer had already accomplished, in anticipation of what they would accomplish together.

Many walked away from their jobs without lengthy deliberation and accepted the often on-the-spot opportunity to work with Dr. Rodgers in what turned out to be a historic transformational health care journey. When invited to participate in this dream mission, these hand-picked professionals signed on, never looking back, some creating decades-long careers at the SUR Health Center. Without these dedicated and talented individuals, much of this story would not be publicly documented nor celebrated or commemorated. My father's admirers ensured the celebrations and the recognition of his milestones along the way. They insisted on the naming of streets, scholarships, and the health center in his name. They fought for the recognition of SUR's cause, as he fought for the rights of all people to have access to health care.

Longtime staff: Clara Maddox, Dr. Samuel Rodgers, Jim Nunnelly

These achievements were not viewed by my father as "photo op fanfare," but as something he simply must do because it was the right thing to do; and who if given this opportunity would not oblige? He cared more about results than accolades, a change agent in every way. Lives were changed in the community where he, with the support of federal funding, made medical access possible and affordable. He replaced hopelessness, frustration, and fear of the health care delivery system with open door opportunities, increasing access for inner city communities of color. He chose not to look the other way at the existing and visible needs left to be addressed. He rescued people from their dire conditions, just as I suspected he was doing in the streets of Anniston as an elementary school boy.

I doubt he ever thought he had everything it took from the very beginning to accomplish all he did, but he remained faithful to his calling. Life opens doors, like flower petals open and unfold in the sun, just when the right time comes. He had no starry-eyed illusions of what others would or might do, nor did he waste time believing racist power structures would make amends on their own, minus actions taken to arrest these indecencies. Instead, without hesitation he pushed forward against many odds without having the final resolution in that moment.

He had always been the one who cared, and this "power of one" awoke a medical community to become a force to be reckoned with. All it took was one who cared enough to strike a match in the forest that set the whole world ablaze. He taught me that we each have the power of conviction to ignite a movement of our choice, with positive outcomes for others, if only we are courageous enough to do so.

ECHOES

There remain echoes of my father everywhere my imagination will take me. I imagine our family at the dinner table enjoying one of my mother's home-cooked meals and each other. One of my father's favorite meals were fried pork chops, rice, and home-made gravy—hold the vegetables please! My father sat at the head of the table next to a wall-mounted phone within reach to quickly respond to calls from expectant mothers, who had a schedule all their own. A large chalkboard covered the adjacent wall where we practiced our multiplication tables and tic-tac-toe, and my father quickly scribbled patients phone numbers. Mostly, he would write notes on the back of his hand.

My father would ask a question or two he already knew the answer to before asking the Three R's the question. One of his favorite stunner questions was, "If a tree falls in the forest and nobody is around to hear it, does it make a sound?" This show-stopping question would end our dinner table shenanigans, although that was not the point. My father's goal, I believe, was to train us to think through a question to formulate a thoughtful response.

Following my father's death, he was the big tree that had fallen in the community "forest" of Kansas City and nationally across the public health community, and everyone heard and felt it. Finally, I could answer that question easily. My father unleashed a health care revolution in the quiet of the day. No fanfare, no boasting, no empty talk. Just truthful, tough talk and a courageous walk, accompanied by direct actions.

"He could raise the correct issues and then have the wherewithal to do something about them," said Jim Nunnelly.

He eased into the rooms of power brokers and spoke on behalf of the people who had been talked over, ignored. He was a pioneer in the health center movement and an unfortunate veteran of the civil rights movement—one he had lived a lifetime.

NACHC HONORS LEADERSHIP

The best judge of character and overall impact resulting from the leadership effectiveness of Dr. Sam Rodgers was reflected through the accolades received from the National Association of Community Health Centers (NACHC), the foremost health center association representing community health centers nationwide. NACHC was founded in 1971 to "promote efficient, high quality, comprehensive health care that is accessible, culturally and linguistically competent, community directed, and patient centered for all." The SURHC opened in 1968 under the leadership of Dr. Sam Rodgers, a man and a vision ahead of its time.

In 1978, NACHC honored Dr. Rodgers with a special award established in his name: the Samuel U. Rodgers Achievement Award for Dedication and Excellence in the Field of Community Health Care Delivery. Upon his retirement,

Tom Van Coverden, president and CEO of NACHC, had the following to say about him:

"Under the leadership of and innovation of Dr. Rodgers, the center has become a prized asset of community working to improve health, provide jobs, and promote greater personal responsibility for good health and prevention."

"The nation owes a debt of gratitude to Dr. Rodgers. He has been a visionary leader advancing health centers as a cost-effective solution to meeting America's growing health needs. Overwhelming passage by Congress of an unprecedented five-year reauthorization of America's health center programs stands as tribute to Dr. Rodgers and others like him, whose achievements demonstrate that public investment in health centers produce substantial returns to the nation in good health, prevention, and cost savings."

"Dr. Rodgers is recognized as a national authority on minority health problems. He is the recipient of high national honor for his outspoken advocacy for the medically underserved and his legendary efforts to break discriminatory barriers for black doctors in the nation's medical schools and hospitals." (NACHLINK. Community Health Pioneer Retires. Winter 1997-Vol. 3, No. 4. James W. Couch)

"The ultimate measure of a man is not where he stands in moments of comfort and convenience, but where he stands at times of challenge and controversy."

DR. MARTIN LUTHER KING, JR.

The Gala and New Horizons

THE FIFTIETH ANNIVERSARY GALA CELEBRATION

The inspiration for my writing journey was my participation in the Samuel U. Rodgers Fiftieth Anniversary Golden Globe Gala on September 15, 2018, in Kansas City—one of many inspirational moments. But the catalytic impact of the gala was my turning point.

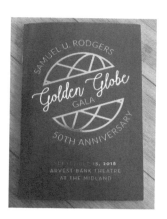

Golden Globe Gala Fiftieth Anniversary Celebration Program

I have acknowledged that we are all a total sum of our parts. Our lives and who we become are an exotic concoction of our birth places, ancestors, family, our migration movements to other geographical areas, schooling, and professional endeavors—all layered atop our personal callings and faults. I wanted to return and relive my excitement of that September night. I would travel back in time to the celebratory place where it all happened, all in my mind. Just the thought of that dazzling evening was exhilarating.

The celebratory venue was the Loew's Midland Theatre, an architectural gem constructed in downtown Kansas City in 1927. The hundreds of people who arrived in formal attire included current and past health center staff, medical colleagues, city, county, and state government officials, family, friends, patients, and corporate sponsors. Senior citizens, as young professionals, were recruited and mentored by Dr. Rodgers. This faithful group of witnesses, some there from the beginning, were honored in a special pre-event function. Many attendees had never met my father. Regardless of past affiliation, they were all there that night in support of my father's vision.

Loew's Midland Theatre staircase

Loew's Midland Theatre stage

Loew's Midland Theatre loge

My sister and I were escorted by an event host to the loge balcony, a secluded pre-reception area of the theatre that overlooked the main theatre floor. As the last two living members of our once five-member family, we are now the sole members left to tell our father's story. We were on the formal program to speak at the event. As the first guests to arrive, we were greeted by a videographer who warmly extended a microphone and simultaneous invitation for impromptu comments. As I began to speak of what my father would think if he were present, my thoughts traveled backward at lightning speed. I was suddenly speechless, overwhelmed by emotion, in a slow-motion free fall of decades of family stories. Below me I envisioned groups of family members, arms outstretched, waiting to break my fall, then returned to reality. What only my sister and I would fully understand was our father's special achievements were not just his alone, but rather a culmination of his family's past achievements.

We carried their collective spirits with us, from Anniston, Alabama, and 18th Street and Vine, as we entered the Loew's Midland Theater that night. The character and achievements of our father were impossible to distill in minutes. We felt the joy and weight of our responsibility simultaneously, and now the moment had arrived.

GALA FIFTIETH ANNIVERSARY HONOREES

My sister and I were whisked from the loge balcony into an adjacent private reception area where the fiftieth anniversary honorees would gather. We were the first to arrive and had been selected to speak to this special group, given ten minutes each and an additional five-minute greeting at the main event. Fifty-three key individuals and twenty-two organizations honorees had been nominated for this pre-gala event. We knew the majority of the honorees from our childhoods, and reading their names was a reliving of the early health center beginnings, brick by brick, person by person. The nominee list was comprised of the living and the dead, including my father's Hospital Hill colleagues, current and past employees, secretaries, nurses, social workers, former board members, accountants, attorneys, doctors, corporate executive directors, janitors, all pioneers who contributed to the mission. The average length of health center service was notably twenty to forty years, a remarkable occurrence. Deeply inspired at the gathering of so many heroes in one place, we glanced knowingly at each other and were handed the microphone. The only one person that was missing was our father.

Daughters Commemoration of SUR (Rosalyn & Rita)

A MESSAGE FROM MYSELF AND DR. RITA RODGERS STANLEY:

"I know that if Dr. Rodgers was here tonight celebrating fifty years of work at the center, he would be so tickled, wondering what all the fuss was about. He would be pleased that so many people have been impacted and empowered by the work that's been done. Given an opportunity to say some words to this audience, he would express thanks and acknowledge the progress made, but then quickly remind us that there is still so much more to do. He would fully expect that we would do whatever was in our power to remove the obstacles that keep us from reaching more people and impacting health outcomes favorably. "

Pre-Reception celebration, Dr. Rita

Giving thought to my sister's last words I stepped forward slowly, taking the mike:

"I imagine what my father would think, were he here tonight. In my father's humbling and quizzical way, he would wear an expression of awe. Not awe in and of himself, but in the presence and turnout of those who are here tonight in celebration of his life and works. The definition of true empathy is to walk a mile in someone's shoes that you've never walked in before. Dr. Rodgers did walk a mile and saw the plight of poverty and inaccessibility in conflict with the basic human right of health care. It is important to take the time to tell someone's story, and maybe one day someone will tell yours.

"Many of you were here from the beginning when the vision was being formed. Many of you are here now in the reformation of this progressive vision to keep it growing strong. We can surround ourselves by the physical manifestation of the health center walls, but what was the heart of the founder, Dr. Rodgers, who first experienced the vision of what health care could be and should be for all? Having your name on a building or street sign is absolutely an honor. But to understand the heart of the pioneer founder is to understand the purpose for which this center began and continues to thrive. My father was more than his achievements and we desire that you learn the fullness of his life. The knowledge of his person is the greater gift."

Rita spoke to the present and future; my speech was more prophetic than I recognized at the time, having no plans whatsoever to write a book. We enjoyed this small gathering surrounded by many familiar faces; it felt like we had come home. We fixed our eyes on each other without another word, knowing we had done our best to represent our father. We hoped he would think so too.

THE MAIN GALA EVENT

The unforgettable celebration included a raffle drawing, live auction, international entertainment, dinner, and the legacy presentation—all activities synchronized by the Masters of Ceremony *KMBC* local news station anchors. The golden globe gala sponsors were many, including anniversary sponsors, Hallmark, LabCorp, Kansas City University of Medicine and Biosciences, and the city of Kansas City, Missouri. In addition, the multi-level donors, totaling eighty-eight in number, included individuals, small businesses, restaurants, news channels, grocers, area hospitals, Kansas City Public Schools, and the KC Royals baseball team, to name a few. All proceeds were purposed to provide patients with compassionate health care.

The program included congratulatory messages from the center's acting health center CEO, the mayor of Kansas City, and Missouri's fifth district congressional representative, Emanuel Cleaver II—all complementary of the efforts of the center. Thousands of dollars were raised in minutes as we dined with the expert guidance of the fastest-talking female auctioneer I had ever witnessed. The Kansas City community showed up in force in support of the center, as they always had.

FOUNDERS' CORE FAMILY BELIEFS

"Tonight's celebration was an acknowledgement of Dr. Rodgers' legacy, and the success of the five health center locations in the KC metro area that currently serves 23,000 patients," announced the KMBC master of ceremony and news anchor from the stage.

Family was everything to my father, and this belief was further emphasized in the gala program. SUR's immediate family and ancestors represented the well of strength and character from which he drank.

The health center's core belief was based on strength of the family, which began with the founder, Dr. Samuel U. Rodgers, MD, MPH. Rodgers believed families deserved access to everything they needed to thrive in the heart of their community. He believed health care is a basic human right, and his vision was to ensure quality, accessible care regardless of your ability to pay. In 1968, Dr. Rodgers was known as the first African American to become a board-certified OB-GYN in the Kansas City area, when he chose to open the health center at the Wayne Miner Housing Project. This center became the first federally funded community health center in Missouri and the fourth of its kind at the time. The SURHC website reads, "Family was the focus of Dr. Rodgers' vision, and it's the family that remains at the heart of the healing work we do today."

And now you know why.

A LEGACY OF SELFLESS DEDICATION

While I had long contemplated documenting my father's legacy, I knew for certain following this gala celebration that I could no longer continue to simply carry these stories solely in my head and heart. I had to document these lessons, not just for the benefit of our immediate family members, but for the good of others who might gain strength from his journey. I considered the long-term dedication of the hundreds who gathered at the gala that night and the numerous people who had contributed to the birth of this vision already gone. I write these triumphant stories connecting the lessons of my family to inspire the lives of others. "This is a story that needs to be told," I was reminded again and again. A story that, as a stranger exclaimed, "belongs to us all."

In sharing the stories that "belong to us all," my writing journey was revelatory in spirit. The seemingly circuitous twists and turns in the process I now acknowledge as kismet-like fate. For years I had collected news articles, photographs, and family memorabilia, never having plans for any of it. I had conducted multiple interviews with family members and health center colleagues and employees who knew my father well. I had not known the enormity of my father's impact, presence, and influence on others until now.

The unburdening of these gifts has been both enlightening and cathartic. I continue to learn about our father and family. I never expected to be so enlightened, with every interview, phone call, and photograph that added new shades to what I thought I had known as my father's story. It was proof that each person held a piece of the puzzle that only they knew. The richness of what was woven together proved more powerful than my beginning memories.

I trust these writings give hope to those who seek truth and purpose in sacrificing for a greater cause. Our father desegregated the hospital system, created one of the first group practices in the US, became one of the first African American board-certified OB-GYNs in Kansas City, and established one of the most renowned health centers in the nation, where respect for patients still comes first.

The selfless dedication to his profession and his advocacy for the medically underserved was widely honored and recognized. Above all, he was a good man.

AWARDS ESTABLISHED
- 1977, established by NACHC: Samuel U. Rodgers, MD Achievement Award
- 2000, established by Missouri Primary Care Association: Samuel U. Rodgers Achievement Award

HONORS RECEIVED
- American Heart Association's Gold Heart Award
- Wayne Miner Health Center officially renamed "Samuel U. Rodgers Health Center"
- 1988 Ambassador of Hope, Award of Courage, American Cancer Society
- Presidents Award, Southern Christian Leadership Conference
- Ivanhoe Public Service Award for Outstanding Achievement in the Field of Human Relations, Ivanhoe Club

POSITIONS HELD
- Executive Director, Samuel U. Rodgers Health Center
- Clinical Professor, Obstetrics/Gynecology, University of Missouri-Kansas City School of Medicine
- Founding Member and Executive Board Member, National Association of Community Health Centers (NACHC)
- Member, Missouri Coalition of Community and Migrant Health Centers

"His compassion and life-long commitment ministering to the needs of fellow human beings have enriched his community and endeared him to many as a man of goodness, mercy, and love. Dr. Rodgers has been at the core of NACHC, actively engaging

teamwork and high standards, which have contributed to the
expansion of health centers across the nation."

JAMES W. COUCH, CHAIR OF THE NACHC BOARD.

TODAY

As for my father's vision? My father had an uncanny ability
to see down the street and around the corner. His dreams
are just rounding the bend and will now be executed by the
"dream carriers," those who are inspired and dedicated to living out in remembrance works that transform a community.

Mr. Jim Nunnelly, a twenty-five-year employee and lifetime
advocate of everything SUR, continues to speak about health
care and community reform, posting often at 3 a.m. about the
innovative approaches established in the beginning. Jim hosts
a weekly radio talk show about health issues and remains
one of the most outspoken proponents of SURHC, sharing
its rich history anytime he is asked.

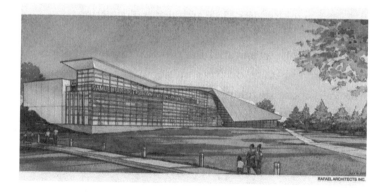

SURHC architectural rendering

Samuel U. Rodgers Health Center now serves over twenty-one thousand patients at four locations throughout the Kansas City area, through the assistance of interpreters speaking thirty-eight languages and a staff of "260 full or part time" employees.

Sam Rodgers Place architectural rendering

The community celebrated the official groundbreaking for Sam Rodgers Place on May 23, 2022. The sixty-two-unit mixed-income development on the Samuel U. Rodgers campus is in the Historic Northeast's Independence Plaza neighborhood, adjacent to the health center. Sam Rodgers Place will provide housing across the income spectrum, representing a unique opportunity to combine housing and health to serve the needs of the families in the community.

(City News, News Release. Sam Rodgers Place, Final Paseo Gateway Phase Breaks Ground. May 20, 2022.)

"Bring health care to the people where they are."
DR. SAMUEL U. RODGERS

Dr. Rita Rodgers Stanley continues the family legacy of compassionate care to the community and advocacy for the poor. Dr. Stanley's private practice in functional medicine is focused on disease prevention and wellness. Dr. Rita is a member of the Rodgers Health Center's board of directors founded by Dr. Samuel U Rodgers over fifty years ago.

A MESSAGE FROM DR. RITA RODGERS STANLEY:
"Looking back on these fifty years, and looking forward to the future of the health center, I say this to my father:

Daddy, all of your sacrifices, your time, your frustrations, and your heart…it's worth it. The seeds you planted while you were here are bearing fruit in the lives of people who have served and been served. Your legacy will continue through the lives of your children and the people who have served and been served. I pray that you rest, knowing that the people you love and the people you put your faith in will continue

the work and assure that your legacy and vision never die."

Acknowledgements

First, I must thank God above all others who always knows my heart. I had not intended to write a book, but only to tell a story. With many prayers forgotten, the book happened as it should have. Thank you for placing me in the care of this family, without whom there would be no story to tell.

I'd like to start by thanking my family for their collective memories of forgotten details and for inspiring my love of stories and storytelling by caring enough to listen.

Thank you to everyone who has been a part of this journey— those who have encouraged me and insisted that this story be shared for the benefit of many and for the sake of history.

To Jim Nunnelly, the constant face of health center history: Thank you for sharing your lived knowledge and willingness to tell these stories with such love, no matter the time or day.

To Jesse J. Spikes, my steadfast partner and sounding board throughout this process: Thanks for your patience and feedback.

To my sister Rita, with whom I share so many memories of our father: I thank you for your love, constant encouragement, and faith in me. I hope these character-based stories exemplified through our ancestors will be a constant reminder to stay the course. Keep the faith in all your endeavors, regardless of how it may look. You have ancestors rooting for you. Thank you for being that personal example of their sacrifice.

A special thanks to the interviewees whose stories I share in my book who have trusted me with their unique passages of history as it occurred. Thank you for this gift.

- General James Hall, Jr.
- Joseph Harkins
- Wilhemenia Ballew Howard
- Clara Maddox
- Jim Nunnelly
- Horace Rodgers
- Dr. David Satcher
- Dr. Rita Rodgers Stanley

To Eric Koester who first encouraged me to join this cohort, and a thank you to the entire New Degree Press team for all you do.

Lastly, the publishing of this book was made possible by a community of family and friends who believed this was a story worthy to tell.

Angeline Miller
Anita Elaine Cox
Ann Dickerson

Arthur E. Pullam IV
Becky Ward
Beverly Rodgers

Bob Theis
Carol Tucker-Burden
Cedrella Jones-Taylor
Cheryl Ransom
Chuck Alexander
Chunxian Li
Claudia Therese Cotton
Damon Bassey
Deborah Combs
DoJuan Hobson Wesley
Donna Jones Badocchi
Effuah Chisholm
Eric Koester
Eric Parker
Faisal Khan
Fern Scott
Frederic G Ransom MD
Gordon A. Rodgers III
Gordon A. Rodgers III
Hassiba Braggs
Helen Davis Hatch
Helga H Oldenkamp
Janet E. Ransom
Janet Justus, Andrea Wickerham
Janet Parker
Jean Hunnicutt
Jeff Parker
Jennine Jackson
Jesse J Spikes
Jifunza Wright
Julian Rodgers
June Joseph Steele

Kathryn Love
Katrina Rodgers
Katrina Walker
Kayla Taylor
Kim Haith
Kimberly Cook
Kimberly Schlichter
Lisa Foy
Lisa Henry Horne
Lisa Rosenbaum
Lynn Fritzlen
Mary McGilley
Mary Scott
Michelle Jones
Michelle Sands
Morris Herndon
Natasha Joplin
Nina Howard
~Nioshii~ Wilde
Pamela Rodgers
Penella Washington
Penny Wright
Quaye Chapman Reed
Rebecca Caldwell
Renee Pryor Newton
Rev. Denise Burriss
Rita Brown
Rita Stanley
Robert C Keene
Rona Green
Rosemarie Jackson
Rossheda McLarin

Sakinah Jones
Shirley Ann Curl
Shontel Ransom
Stephanie Brooks
Stephanie Ray
Tananjalyn Wilson
Thomas Rafalsky
Tina Allen
Ulrica Wilson
Wendell Love
Zarita Pearson

Appendix

AUTHOR'S NOTE:

Hunter, Glen, Robin Silverman, John Simonson, and Philip Stephens. "Heaven-sent. Local Heroes Glorify Kansas City." *Ingram's,* December 1996, 35.

Ly, Daniel P. "Historical Trends in the Representativeness and Incomes of Black Physicians." *Journal of General Internal Medicine,* April 2022. https://doi.org/10.1007/s11606-021-06745-1.

Merriam-Webster. s.v. "zero-sum game." Accessed June 7, 2022. https://www.merriam-webster.com/dictionary/zero-sum%20 game.game.

PART 1: EARLY LIFE AND EDUCATION (1850 –1942)

CHAPTER 1: THE SEED

Welchel Jr., L.H. *The History and Heritage of African American Churches: A Way Out of No Way.* St. Paul: Paragon House, 2011.

CHAPTER 3: THE RODGERS ENCLAVE

Allen, James. *As A Man Thinketh*. New York City: TarcherPerigee, 1902.

Morgan, Tee. *Annie's Town Revisited: A Picture History of Anniston, Alabama*. Anniston: Ralph Higginbotham, 1990.

CHAPTER 4: FIRST FAMILY

Cassedy, James Gilbert. "African Americans and the American Labor Movement." *Prologue Magazine: Federal Records and African American History*, Summer 1997. https://www.archives.gov/publications/prologue/1997/summer/american-labor-movement.html.

CHAPTER 5: JIM CROW SOUTH EDUCATION

AL.com. "More than 300 African-Americans Lynched in Alabama in 66 Years." AL.com press release, April 26, 2018. https://www.al.com/news/2018/04/alabamas_racial_lynching_victi.html.

Harley, Earl.H. *The Forgotten History of Defunct Medical Schools in the 19th and 20th Centuries and the Impact of the Flexner Report*. Washington, District of Columbia: Journal of the National Medical Association, 2006. Accessed June 6, 2022. https://www.ncbi.nlm.nih.gov.

History. "How the GI Bill's Promise Was Denied to a Million Black WWII Veterans." *History Stories*. Updated April 20, 2021. https://www.history.com/news/gi-bill-black-wwii-veterans-benefits.

History. "Why Harry Truman Ended Segregation in the US Military in 1948." *History Stories*. November 5, 2020. https://www.history.com/news/harry-truman-executive-order-9981-desegration-military-1948.

History News Network. "The Dred Scott Case Said Blacks Had No Rights the 'White Man Was Bound to Respect.' But in the West Things Turned Out Differently." History News Network press release, March 8, 2015. https://historynewsnetwork.org/article/158681.

National Park Service. "Brown v. Board of Education of Topeka Kansas." Updated April 1, 2016. https://www.nps.gov/articles/brown-v-board-of-education.htm.

Talladega College. "Talladega College - Our History." *Our History*. Accessed May 2022. https://www.talledega.edu/our-history/.

The National WWII Museum, New Orleans. "Death of the Duce, Benito Mussolini." *The War*. April 28, 2020. https://www.nationalww2museum.org/death-of-benito-mussolini.

PART 2: MIDWEST MIGRATION (1942–1950)

CHAPTER 2: GENERAL HOSPITAL NO. 2

Rodgers, Samuel U. "KANSAS CITY GENERAL HOSPITAL – A Historical Summary." *Journal of the National Medical Association*, no. 54, (1962): 525–639. https://www.jnma00687-0005.pdfnih.gov.

CHAPTER 3: HOSPITAL HILL DESEGREGATION

Cassedy, James Gilbert. "African Americans and the American Labor Movement." *Prologue Magazine: Federal Records and African American History*, Summer 1997. https://www.archives.gov/publications/prologue/1997/summer/american-labor-movement.html.

Rodgers, Samuel U. "Kansas City General Hospital - A Historical Summary." *Journal of the National Medical Association*, no. 54, (1962): 534–535. https://www.jnma00687-0005.pdf (nih.gov).

PART 3: THE GOOD LIFE (1950–1965)

CHAPTER 1: PRACTICE MAKES PERFECT

"Dr. Samuel U. Rodgers Passes American Board." *The Kansas City Star*, 1953.

Johnson, James S. "The Kansas City Medical Society." *Journal of the National Medical Association*, no. 54, (1962): 539–540. https://www.ncbi.nlm.nih.gov/pmc/articles/PMC2642144/pdf/jnma00687-0005.pdf.

"VOTE IN NEGRO DOCTORS - Inter-Racial Milestone." *The Kansas City Star*, October 24, 1950.

Williams, Dr. Starks. "AS I SEE IT - Integration of KC Hospitals Was a Slow Process." *The Kansas City Star*.

CHAPTER 2: THE MIRACLE

Maria, Madeline Sister. "Queen of The World Hospital." *Journal of the National Medical Association*, no. 54, (1962): 537–539. https://www.jnmao0687-0005.pdf (nih.gov).

Maryknoll. *Maryknoll, a catholic nonprofit mission movement...*, 2022. https://www.maryknoll.org/.

"NO MEDICAL BAR - TO MARYKNOLL ORDER." *The Kansas City Times*, May 23, 1955.

Rodgers, Samuel U. "KANSAS CITY GENERAL HOSPITAL - A Historical Summary." *Journal of the National Medical Association*, no. 54, (1962): 534–535. https://www.jnmao0687-0005.pdf (nih.gov).

CHAPTER 3: SIMPLY THE BEST

Rodgers, Samuel U. "KANSAS CITY GENERAL HOSPITAL-A Historical Summary." *Journal of the National Medical Association*, no. 54 (1962):543. https://www.jnmao0687-0005.pdf (nih.gov).

"WILL OPEN NEW CLINIC - DOCTORS GROUP PLANS EVENT NEXT SUNDAY." *The Kansas City Star*, February 5, 1961.

CHAPTER 4: THE GOOD FIGHT

Noble, Phil. *BEYOND the BURNING BUS: The Civil Rights Revolution In A Southern Town.* Montgomery: NewSouth Books, 2003, 89.

Nelson, Stanley, dir. *Freedom Riders*. 2010; Arlington, Massachusetts: American Experience Films. DVD, 117 mins.

Noble, Phil. *Beyond the Burning Bus: The Civil Rights Revolution In A Southern Town*. Montgomery: NewSouth Books, 2003, 131.

Noble, Phil. *Beyond the Burning Bus: The Civil Rights Revolution In A Southern Town*. Montgomery: NewSouth Books, 2003, 126.

Rodgers, Gordon A. "Gordon Rodgers Obituary." *The Birmingham News, December 27, 2007.* https://obits.al.com/us/obituaries/birmingham/name/gordon-rodgers-obituary?id=13181055.

PART 4: THE VISION (1965—1996)

CHAPTER 1: THE CALLING

History.com Editors. "1967 Detroit Riots." *Topics - Race in America*. Updated March 23, 2021. https://www.history.com/topics/1960s/1967-detroit-riots.

Oxford's Learners Dictionaries. s.v. "anomaly." Accessed June 21, 2022. https://www.oxfordlearnersdictionaries.com/us/definition/english/anomaly?q=anomaly.

CHAPTER 2: HEALTH AND TRANSFORMATION

Collins, Jim. GOOD TO GREAT. New York NY: Harper Collins, 2001.

CHAPTER 6: THE RENAMING

Hassanein, Nada. "Health of Black, Native Moms Key In Fight to Improve Infant Death Disparities, Experts Say." *USA TODAY*, December 11, 2021. https://www.usatoday.com/story/news/health/2021/12/11/deaths-black-babies-marker-systemic-racism-experts-say/6417090001/.

Novoa, Christina and Jamila Taylor. "Exploring African Americans' High Maternal and Infant Death Rates." *CAP Report*, February 1, 2018. https://www.americanprogress.org/article/exploring-african-americans-high-maternal-infant-death-rates/.

CHAPTER 7: LIKE FATHER, LIKE DAUGHTER

Montgomery, Rick. "Doctor Sees Reality of Poor Daily." *The Kansas City Star*, September 2, 1990.

PART 5: THE SUNSET (1996–1999)

CHAPTER 1: THE JOURNEY AT SUNSET

Bedford, Melissa. "FOLLOWING FATHERS FOOTSTEPS." *The Kansas City Star-Business*, April 5, 1996.

Couch, James. "Community Health Pioneer Retires." *NACHCLINK*, Winter 1997: 6.

Douglas, Debbie. "The Story Behind Photo! I've photographed many Presidents, but this story is about Dr. Samuel U. Rodgers and what a great man he was! Also, how I was able to get..." *Facebook*, February 10, 2021. https://m.facebook.com/

photo.php?fbid=10221939051924508&id=1205854675&se
t=a.1010964793482&source=57&refid=52&tn=EHH-R.

"Dr. Rita Rodgers-Stanley Named Permanent Head of Rodgers
Community Health Center." *THE CALL - Southwest's Leading Weekly*, December 6, 1996.

Hunter, Glen, Robin Silverman, John Simonson, and Philip
Stephens. "Heaven-sent. Local Heroes Glorify Kansas City."
Ingram's, December 1996, 35.

"NO MEDICAL BAR—TO MARYKNOLL ORDER." *The
Kansas City Times*, May 23, 1955.

Thurman, Howard. *Meditations of the Heart*. New York: Harper
& Row, 1953.

CHAPTER 6: LEADERSHIP SUR STYLE
Couch, James. "Community Health Pioneer Retires." *NACH-
CLINK*, Winter 1997: 6.

CHAPTER 7: THE GALA AND NEW HORIZONS
Samuel U. Rodgers Health Center. "OUR FOUNDER'S
STORY." *WHO WE ARE*, May 2022. https://samrodgers.org/
who-we-are/#pageSection2.

Made in United States
Troutdale, OR
09/30/2024

23257568R00186